MznLnx

Missing Links Exam Preps

Exam Prep for

Customer Behavior: A Managerial Perspective

Sheth & Mittal, 2nd Edition

The MznLnx Exam Prep is your link from the texbook and lecture to your exams.
The MznLnx Exam Preps are unauthorized and comprehensive reviews of your textbooks.

All material provided by MznLnx and Rico Publications (c) 2010
Textbook publishers and textbook authors do not particpate in or contribute to these reviews.

MznLnx

Rico
Publications

Exam Prep for Customer Behavior: A Managerial Perspective
2nd Edition
Sheth & Mittal

Publisher: Raymond Houge
Assistant Editor: Michael Rouger
Text and Cover Designer: Lisa Buckner
Marketing Manager: Sara Swagger
Project Manager, Editorial Production: Jerry Emerson
Art Director: Vernon Lowerui

Product Manager: Dave Mason
Editorial Assitant: Rachel Guzmanji
Pedagogy: Debra Long
Cover Image: Jim Reed/Getty Images
Text and Cover Printer: City Printing, Inc.
Compositor: Media Mix, Inc.

(c) 2010 Rico Publications
ALL RIGHTS RESERVED. No part of this work covered by the copyright may be reproduced or used in any form or by an means--graphic, electronic, or mechanical, including photocopying, recording, taping, Web distribution, information storage, and retrieval systems, or in any other manner--without the written permission of the publisher.

Printed in the United States
ISBN:

For more information about our products, contact us at:
Dave.Mason@RicoPublications.com

For permission to use material from this text or product, submit a request online to:
Dave.Mason@RicoPublications.com

Contents

CHAPTER 1
The Customer: Key to Market Success — 1

CHAPTER 2
Determinants of Customer Behavior: Personal Factors and Market Environment — 9

CHAPTER 3
Trends in Determinants of Customer Behavior — 22

CHAPTER 4
The Customer as a Perceiver and Learner — 29

CHAPTER 5
Customer Motivation: Needs, Emotions, and Psychographics — 37

CHAPTER 6
Customer Attitudes: Cognitive and Affective — 44

CHAPTER 7
Researching Customer Behavior — 49

CHAPTER 8
Individual Customer Decision Making — 59

CHAPTER 9
Institution Customer Decision Making: Household, Business, and Government — 65

CHAPTER 10
Relationship-Based Buying — 73

CHAPTER 11
Customer Loyalty to Products, Brands, and Stores — 78

CHAPTER 12
Online Customer Behavior — 85

CHAPTER 13
Creating Market Values for the Customer — 92

ANSWER KEY — 99

TO THE STUDENT

COMPREHENSIVE

The *MznLnx* Exam Prep series is designed to help you pass your exams. Editors at MznLnx review your textbooks and then prepare these practice exams to help you master the textbook material. Unlike study guides, workbooks, and practice tests provided by the texbook publisher and textbook authors, *MznLnx* gives you **all** of the material in each chapter in exam form, not just samples, so you can be sure to nail your exam.

MECHANICAL

The MznLnx Exam Prep series creates exams that will help you learn the subject matter as well as test you on your understanding. Each question is designed to help you master the concept. Just working through the exams, you gain an understanding of the subject--its a simple mechanical process that produces success.

INTEGRATED STUDY GUIDE AND REVIEW

MznLnx is not just a set of exams designed to test you, its also a comprehensive review of the subject content. Each exam question is also a review of the concept, making sure that you will get the answer correct without having to go to other sources of material. You learn as you go! Its the easiest way to pass an exam.

HUMOR

Studying can be tedious and dry. MznLnx's instructional design includes moderate humor within the exam questions on occassion, to break the tedium and revitalize the brain

Chapter 1. The Customer: Key to Market Success

1. _____ is the study of when, why, how, where and what people do or do not buy products. It blends elements from psychology, sociology, social psychology, anthropology and economics. It attempts to understand the buyer decision making process, both individually and in groups. It studies characteristics of individual consumers such as demographics and behavioural variables in an attempt to understand people's wants. It also tries to assess influences on the consumer from groups such as family, friends, reference groups, and society in general.

   a. Consumer confidence
   b. Communal marketing
   c. Consumer behavior
   d. Multidimensional scaling

2. _____ is defined by the American _____ Association as the activity, set of institutions, and processes for creating, communicating, delivering, and exchanging offerings that have value for customers, clients, partners, and society at large. The term developed from the original meaning which referred literally to going to market, as in shopping, or going to a market to sell goods or services.

   _____ practice tends to be seen as a creative industry, which includes advertising, distribution and selling.

   a. Customer acquisition management
   b. Product naming
   c. Marketing
   d. Marketing myopia

3. _____ is difficult to define. For example, in 1952, Alfred Kroeber and Clyde Kluckhohn compiled a list of 164 definitions of '_____' in _____: A Critical Review of Concepts and Definitions. However, the word '_____' is most commonly used in three basic senses:

   - excellence of taste in the fine arts and humanities
   - an integrated pattern of human knowledge, belief, and behavior that depends upon the capacity for symbolic thought and social learning
   - the set of shared attitudes, values, goals, and practices that characterizes an institution, organization or group.

   When the concept first emerged in eighteenth- and nineteenth-century Europe, it connoted a process of cultivation or improvement, as in agriculture or horticulture. In the nineteenth century, it came to refer first to the betterment or refinement of the individual, especially through education, and then to the fulfillment of national aspirations or ideals.

   a. African Americans
   b. Albert Einstein
   c. AStore
   d. Culture

Chapter 1. The Customer: Key to Market Success

4. _____ is the collection, deployment and translation of information that allows a business to acquire, develop and retain their customers.

Firslty, the collected data must be audited to fully understand the quality and opportunity within the database. Once this is done, there are a number of different types of analysis that can be applied.

   a. Societal marketing
   b. Customer insight
   c. Customer analytics
   d. Fifth screen

5. In economics, business, retail, and accounting, a _____ is the value of money that has been used up to produce something, and hence is not available for use anymore. In economics, a _____ is an alternative that is given up as a result of a decision. In business, the _____ may be one of acquisition, in which case the amount of money expended to acquire it is counted as _____.
   a. Cost
   b. Transaction cost
   c. Variable cost
   d. Fixed costs

6. Competitiveness is a comparative concept of the ability and performance of a firm, sub-sector or country to sell and supply goods and/or services in a given market. Although widely used in economics and business management, the usefulness of the concept, particularly in the context of national competitiveness, is vigorously disputed by economists, such as Paul Krugman.

The term may also be applied to markets, where it is used to refer to the extent to which the market structure may be regarded as perfectly _____.

   a. Customs union
   b. Competitive
   c. Geographical pricing
   d. Free trade zone

7. _____ is, in very basic words, a position a firm occupies against its competitors.

According to Michael Porter, the three methods for creating a sustainable _____ are through:

1. Cost leadership - Cost advantage occurs when a firm delivers the same services as its competitors but at a lower cost;

2.

   a. 180SearchAssistant
   b. 6-3-5 Brainwriting
   c. Power III
   d. Competitive advantage

8. _____ in economics and business is the result of an exchange and from that trade we assign a numerical monetary value to a good, service or asset. If I trade 4 apples for an orange, the _____ of an orange is 4 - apples. Inversely, the _____ of an apple is 1/4 oranges.

   a. Pricing
   b. Contribution margin-based pricing
   c. Discounts and allowances
   d. Price

9. _____ is a reference to the passing of information from person to person. Originally the term referred specifically to oral communication (literally words from the mouth), but now includes any type of human communication, such as face to face, telephone, email, and text messaging.

Word-of-mouth marketing, which encompasses a variety of subcategories, including buzz, blog, viral, grassroots, cause influencers and social media marketing, as well as ambassador programs, work with consumer-generated media and more, can be highly valued by product marketers.

   a. Marketing communication
   b. New Media Strategies
   c. Merchandise
   d. Word of mouth

10. _____ is the examining of goods or services from retailers with the intent to purchase at that time. _____ is an activity of selection and/or purchase. In some contexts it is considered a leisure activity as well as an economic one.

   a. Discount store
   b. Shopping
   c. Hawkers
   d. Khodebshchik

11. _____ is a broad label that refers to any individuals or households that use goods and services generated within the economy. The concept of a _____ is used in different contexts, so that the usage and significance of the term may vary.

A _____ is a person who uses any product or service.

   a. Consumer
   b. Power III
   c. 6-3-5 Brainwriting
   d. 180SearchAssistant

12. The process of _____ involves the introduction of a good or service that is new or substantially improved. This includes, but is not limited to, improvements in functional characteristics, technical abilities, or ease of use.
   a. Service-profit chain
   b. Teaser rate
   c. Discontinuation
   d. Product innovation

13. _____ is the price at which an asset would trade in a competitive Walrasian auction setting. _____ is often used interchangeably with open _____, fair value or fair _____, although these terms have distinct definitions in different standards, and may differ in some circumstances.

International Valuation Standards defines _____ as 'the estimated amount for which a property should exchange on the date of valuation between a willing buyer and a willing seller in an arm's-length transaction after proper marketing wherein the parties had each acted knowledgeably, prudently, and without compulsion.'

_____ is a concept distinct from market price, which is 'the price at which one can transact', while _____ is 'the true underlying value' according to theoretical standards.

   a. Restructuring
   b. Power III
   c. 180SearchAssistant
   d. Market value

14. _____ is an advertisement in which a particular product specifically mentions a competitor by name for the express purpose of showing why the competitor is inferior to the product naming it.

Chapter 1. The Customer: Key to Market Success

This should not be confused with parody advertisements, where a fictional product is being advertised for the purpose of poking fun at the particular advertisement, nor should it be confused with the use of a coined brand name for the purpose of comparing the product without actually naming an actual competitor. ('Wikipedia tastes better and is less filling than the Encyclopedia Galactica.')

In the 1980s, during what has been referred to as the cola wars, soft-drink manufacturer Pepsi ran a series of advertisements where people, caught on hidden camera, in a blind taste test, chose Pepsi over rival Coca-Cola.

  a. Heavy-up
  b. GL-70
  c. Cost per conversion
  d. Comparative advertising

15. A personal and cultural _____ is a relative ethic _____, an assumption upon which implementation can be extrapolated. A _____ system is a set of consistent _____s and measures that is soo not true. A principle _____ is a foundation upon which other _____s and measures of integrity are based.

  a. Perceptual maps
  b. Package-on-Package
  c. Supreme Court of the United States
  d. Value

16. In algebra, a _____ is a function depending on n that associates a scalar, det(A), to an n×n square matrix A. The fundamental geometric meaning of a _____ is a scale factor for measure when A is regarded as a linear transformation. _____s are important both in calculus, where they enter the substitution rule for several variables, and in multilinear algebra.

For a fixed nonnegative integer n, there is a unique _____ function for the n×n matrices over any commutative ring R. In particular, this function exists when R is the field of real or complex numbers.

  a. Determinant
  b. Black Friday
  c. Package-on-Package
  d. Motion Picture Association of America's film-rating system

17. _____ is the set of reasons that determines one to engage in a particular behavior. The term is generally used for human _____ but, theoretically, it can be used to describe the causes for animal behavior as well

a. Role playing
b. Power III
c. Motivation
d. 180SearchAssistant

18. _____ is a term used in marketing as well as the title of an important marketing paper written by Theodore Levitt. This paper was first published in 1960 in the Harvard Business Review; a journal of which he was an editor.

Some commentators have suggested that its publication marked the beginning of the modern marketing movement.

a. Corporate image
b. Marketing myopia
c. Marketing performance measurement and management
d. Business marketing

19. _____ can be regarded as an outcome of mental processes (cognitive process) leading to the selection of a course of action among several alternatives. Every _____ process produces a final choice. The output can be an action or an opinion of choice.

a. 180SearchAssistant
b. Decision making
c. Power III
d. 6-3-5 Brainwriting

20. A _____ is a set of consistent ethic values (more specifically the personal and cultural values) and measures used for the purpose of ethical or ideological integrity. A well defined _____ is a moral code.

One or more people can hold a _____.

a. 6-3-5 Brainwriting
b. 180SearchAssistant
c. Power III
d. Value system

21. _____ is anything that is intended to save time, energy or frustration. A _____ store at a petrol station, for example, sells items that have nothing to do with gasoline/petrol, but it saves the consumer from having to go to a grocery store. '_____' is a very relative term and its meaning tends to change over time.

a. MaxDiff
b. Convenience
c. Marketing buzz
d. Demographic profile

22. On an intranet or B2E Enterprise Web portals, personalization is often based on user attributes such as department, functional area, or role. The term _____ in this context refers to the ability of users to modify the page layout or specify what content should be displayed.

There are two categories of personalizations:

1. Rule-based
2. Content-based

Web personalization models include rules-based filtering, based on 'if this, then that' rules processing, and collaborative filtering, which serves relevant material to customers by combining their own personal preferences with the preferences of like-minded others. Collaborative filtering works well for books, music, video, etc.

a. Self branding
b. Movin'
c. Cashmere Agency
d. Customization

23. _____ or personalisation is tailoring a consumer product, electronic or written medium to a user based on personal details or characteristics they provide. More recently, it has especially been applied in the context of the World Wide Web.

Web pages are personalized based on the interests of an individual.

a. Sexism,
b. Flighting
c. Personalization
d. Complex sale

24. Maslow's _____ is a theory in psychology, proposed by Abraham Maslow in his 1943 paper A Theory of Human Motivation, which he subsequently extended to include his observations of humans' innate curiosity.

Chapter 1. The Customer: Key to Market Success

Maslow studied what he called exemplary people such as Albert Einstein, Jane Addams, Eleanor Roosevelt, and Frederick Douglass rather than mentally ill or neurotic people, writing that 'the study of crippled, stunted, immature, and unhealthy specimens can yield only a cripple psychology and a cripple philosophy.' Maslow also studied the healthiest one percent of the college student population. In his book, The Farther Reaches of Human Nature, Maslow writes, 'By ordinary standards of this kind of laboratory research...

a. Hierarchy of needs
b. 6-3-5 Brainwriting
c. Power III
d. 180SearchAssistant

25. _____ is the term used to describe a situation where different entities cooperate advantageously for a final outcome. Simply defined, it means that the whole is greater than the sum of its parts. The essence of _____ is to value differences.
    a. Power III
    b. 6-3-5 Brainwriting
    c. Synergy
    d. 180SearchAssistant

26. In probability theory and statistics, the _____ of a random variable, probability distribution, or sample is a measure of statistical dispersion, averaging the squared distance of its possible values from the expected value (mean.) Whereas the mean is a way to describe the location of a distribution, the _____ is a way to capture its scale or degree of being spread out. The unit of _____ is the square of the unit of the original variable.
    a. Standard deviation
    b. Correlation
    c. Variance
    d. Sample size

Chapter 2. Determinants of Customer Behavior: Personal Factors and Market Environment

1. _____ is the study of when, why, how, where and what people do or do not buy products. It blends elements from psychology, sociology,social psychology, anthropology and economics. It attempts to understand the buyer decision making process, both individually and in groups. It studies characteristics of individual consumers such as demographics and behavioural variables in an attempt to understand people's wants. It also tries to assess influences on the consumer from groups such as family, friends, reference groups, and society in general.
    a. Multidimensional scaling
    b. Communal marketing
    c. Consumer confidence
    d. Consumer behavior

2. In algebra, a _____ is a function depending on n that associates a scalar, det(A), to an n×n square matrix A. The fundamental geometric meaning of a _____ is a scale factor for measure when A is regarded as a linear transformation. _____s are important both in calculus, where they enter the substitution rule for several variables, and in multilinear algebra.

    For a fixed nonnegative integer n, there is a unique _____ function for the n×n matrices over any commutative ring R. In particular, this function exists when R is the field of real or complex numbers.

    a. Package-on-Package
    b. Motion Picture Association of America's film-rating system
    c. Black Friday
    d. Determinant

3. _____ has been defined by the International Organization for Standardization (ISO) as 'ensuring that information is accessible only to those authorized to have access' and is one of the cornerstones of information security. _____ is one of the design goals for many cryptosystems, made possible in practice by the techniques of modern cryptography.

    _____ also refers to an ethical principle associated with several professions (e.g., medicine, law, religion, professional psychology, and journalism.)

    a. 6-3-5 Brainwriting
    b. 180SearchAssistant
    c. Power III
    d. Confidentiality

4. The nature versus _____ debates concern the relative importance of an individual's innate qualities ('nature', i.e. nativism, or innatism) versus personal experiences ('_____', i.e. empiricism or behaviorism) in determining or causing individual differences in physical and behavioral traits.

Chapter 2. Determinants of Customer Behavior: Personal Factors and Market Environment

The view that humans acquire all or almost all their behavioral traits from '_____' is known as tabula rasa ('blank slate'.) This question was once considered to be an appropriate division of developmental influences, but since both types of factors are known to play such interacting roles in development, many modern psychologists consider the question naive - representing an outdated state of knowledge.

  a. 180SearchAssistant
  b. Nurture
  c. Power III
  d. 6-3-5 Brainwriting

5. The _____ is a term coined by journalist Tom Brokaw to describe the generation of Americans who grew up during the deprivation of the Great Depression, and then went on to fight in World War II, as well as those whose productivity within the war's home front made a decisive material contribution to the war effort. Some of those who survived the war then went on to build and rebuild United States industries in the years following the war. It follows the Lost Generation of the 1880s who fought in WWI, and precedes the Silent Generation of the 1930s.
  a. Greatest Generation
  b. Generation Y
  c. AStore
  d. Generation X

6. _____ is a term used to describe a person who was born during the demographic Post-World War II baby boom. Many analysts now believe that two distinct cultural generations were born during this baby boom; the older generation is often called the Baby Boom Generation and the younger generation is often called Generation Jones. The term '_____' is sometimes used in a cultural context, and sometimes used to describe someone who was born during the post-WWII baby boom.
  a. AStore
  b. Greatest Generation
  c. Generation X
  d. Baby Boomer

7. _____ is a term used to identify people born after the post-World War II increase in birth rates (the baby boom) The term has been used in demography, the social sciences, and marketing, though it is most often used in popular culture.

In the U.S. _____ was originally referred to as the 'baby bust' generation because of the drop in the birth rate following the baby boom.

In the UK the term was first used in a 1964 study of British youth by Jane Deverson.

Chapter 2. Determinants of Customer Behavior: Personal Factors and Market Environment

a. AStore
b. Generation X
c. Generation Y
d. Greatest Generation

8. _____ is a cohort which consists of those people born after the Generation X cohort. Its name is controversial and is synonymous with several alternative names including The Net Generation, Millennials, Echo Boomers, and iGeneration. _____ consists primarily of the offspring of the Generation Jones and Baby Boomers cohorts.
  a. Generation X
  b. Generation Y
  c. AStore
  d. Greatest Generation

9. The _____ was a worldwide economic downturn starting in most places in 1929 and ending at different times in the 1930s or early 1940s for different countries. It was the largest and most important economic depression in the 20th century, and is used in the 21st century as an example of how far the world's economy can fall. The _____ originated in the United States; historians most often use as a starting date the stock market crash on October 29, 1929, known as Black Tuesday.
  a. Power III
  b. 180SearchAssistant
  c. 6-3-5 Brainwriting
  d. Great Depression

10. The name _____ was coined in the November 5, 1951 cover story of Time to refer to the generation coming of age at the time, born during the Great Depression or World War II. The article, , found its characteristics as grave and fatalistic, conventional, possessing confused morals, expecting disappointment but desiring faith, and for women, desiring both a career and a family
  a. Silent Generation
  b. 6-3-5 Brainwriting
  c. Power III
  d. 180SearchAssistant

11. Electronic commerce, commonly known as _____ or eCommerce, consists of the buying and selling of products or services over electronic systems such as the Internet and other computer networks. The amount of trade conducted electronically has grown extraordinarily with wide-spread Internet usage. A wide variety of commerce is conducted in this way, spurring and drawing on innovations in electronic funds transfer, supply chain management, Internet marketing, online transaction processing, electronic data interchange (EDI), inventory management systems, and automated data collection systems.

a. AMAX
b. E-commerce
c. ACNielsen
d. ADTECH

12. _____ is the collection, deployment and translation of information that allows a business to acquire, develop and retain their customers.

Firslty, the collected data must be audited to fully understand the quality and opportunity within the database. Once this is done, there are a number of different types of analysis that can be applied.

a. Fifth screen
b. Societal marketing
c. Customer insight
d. Customer analytics

13. _____ is the generation of people living in Western or First World cultures, born between the mid-1990s and through the 2000s. Following Generation Y, they are typically the children of the youngest Baby Boomers, Generation X and Cold Y Generation The New Silent Generation, related terms, began in 2001.

a. Test market
b. Power III
c. 180SearchAssistant
d. Generation Z

14. Generation Y is a term used to describe the demographic cohort following Generation X. Its members are often referred to as 'Millennials' or '_____') . There are no precise dates for when Gen Y begins and ends. Most commentators use dates from mid 1980s to early 1990s.

a. ADTECH
b. Echo Boomers
c. ACNielsen
d. AMAX

15. In Freudian psychoanalytic theory, defence mechanisms or _____ are psychological strategies brought into play by various entities to cope with reality and to maintain self-image. Healthy persons normally use different defences throughout life. An ego defence mechanism becomes pathological only when its persistent use leads to maladaptive behavior such that the physical and/or mental health of the individual is adversely affected.

a. Defense mechanisms
b. Power III
c. 6-3-5 Brainwriting
d. 180SearchAssistant

16. _____ is difficult to define. For example, in 1952, Alfred Kroeber and Clyde Kluckhohn compiled a list of 164 definitions of '_____' in _____: A Critical Review of Concepts and Definitions. However, the word '_____' is most commonly used in three basic senses:

- excellence of taste in the fine arts and humanities
- an integrated pattern of human knowledge, belief, and behavior that depends upon the capacity for symbolic thought and social learning
- the set of shared attitudes, values, goals, and practices that characterizes an institution, organization or group.

When the concept first emerged in eighteenth- and nineteenth-century Europe, it connoted a process of cultivation or improvement, as in agriculture or horticulture. In the nineteenth century, it came to refer first to the betterment or refinement of the individual, especially through education, and then to the fulfillment of national aspirations or ideals.

a. Albert Einstein
b. African Americans
c. AStore
d. Culture

17. _____ is the process by which a person learns the requirements of the culture by which he or she is surrounded, and acquires values and behaviours that are appropriate or necessary in that culture. The influences which as part of this process limit, direct or shape the individual, whether deliberately of not, include parents, other adults, and peers. If successful, _____ results in competence in the language, values and rituals of the culture.

a. AMAX
b. ADTECH
c. ACNielsen
d. Enculturation

18. In sociology, anthropology and cultural studies, a _____ is a group of people with a culture (whether distinct or hidden) which differentiates them from the larger culture to which they belong. If a particular _____ is characterized by a systematic opposition to the dominant culture, it may be described as a counterculture. As Ken Gelder notes, _____s are social, with their own shared conventions, values and rituals, but they can also seem 'immersed' or self-absorbed--another feature that distinguishes them from countercultures.

Chapter 2. Determinants of Customer Behavior: Personal Factors and Market Environment

   a. 180SearchAssistant
   b. Power III
   c. 6-3-5 Brainwriting
   d. Subculture

19. A personal and cultural _____ is a relative ethic _____, an assumption upon which implementation can be extrapolated. A _____ system is a set of consistent _____s and measures that is soo not true. A principle _____ is a foundation upon which other _____s and measures of integrity are based.
   a. Package-on-Package
   b. Perceptual maps
   c. Value
   d. Supreme Court of the United States

20. A _____ is a commercial building for storage of goods. _____s are used by manufacturers, importers, exporters, wholesalers, transport businesses, customs, etc. They are usually large plain buildings in industrial areas of cities and towns.
   a. Warehouse
   b. 6-3-5 Brainwriting
   c. Power III
   d. 180SearchAssistant

21. A _____ is a retail store, usually selling a wide variety of merchandise, in which customers pay annual membership fees in order to shop. The clubs are able to keep prices low due to the no-frills format of the stores. In addition, customers are required to buy large, wholesale quantities of the store's products, which makes these clubs attractive to both bargain hunters and small business owners.
   a. Self service
   b. Consignment
   c. Warehouse club
   d. Power centre

22. A _____ is a sociological concept referring to a group to which an individual or another group is compared.

   _____s are used in order to evaluate and determine the nature of a given individual or other group's characteristics and sociological attributes. It is the group to which the individual relates or aspires relate himself or self psychologically.

Chapter 2. Determinants of Customer Behavior: Personal Factors and Market Environment

a. Mociology
b. Power III
c. Reference group
d. Minority

23. The _____ is a marketing term and refers to all of the forces outside of marketing that affect marketing management's ability to build and maintain successful relationships with target customers. The _____ consists of both the macroenvironment and the microenvironment.

The microenvironment refers to the forces that are close to the company and affect its ability to serve its customers.

a. Market environment
b. Customer franchise
c. Business-to-consumer
d. Psychographic

24. _____ is the study of the Earth and its lands, features, inhabitants, and phenomena. A literal translation would be 'to describe or write about the Earth'. The first person to use the word '_____' was Eratosthenes.

a. 6-3-5 Brainwriting
b. 180SearchAssistant
c. Power III
d. Geography

25. _____ is a broad label that refers to any individuals or households that use goods and services generated within the economy. The concept of a _____ is used in different contexts, so that the usage and significance of the term may vary.

A _____ is a person who uses any product or service.

a. Power III
b. 6-3-5 Brainwriting
c. 180SearchAssistant
d. Consumer

Chapter 2. Determinants of Customer Behavior: Personal Factors and Market Environment

26. _____ is defined by the American _____ Association as the activity, set of institutions, and processes for creating, communicating, delivering, and exchanging offerings that have value for customers, clients, partners, and society at large. The term developed from the original meaning which referred literally to going to market, as in shopping, or going to a market to sell goods or services.

_____ practice tends to be seen as a creative industry, which includes advertising, distribution and selling.

a. Marketing myopia
b. Customer acquisition management
c. Marketing
d. Product naming

27. The term _____ refers to economy-wide fluctuations in production or economic activity over several months or years. These fluctuations occur around a long-term growth trend, and typically involve shifts over time between periods of relatively rapid economic growth (expansion or boom), and periods of relative stagnation or decline (contraction or recession.)

These fluctuations are often measured using the growth rate of real gross domestic product.

a. Perfect competition
b. Market structure
c. Monopolistic competition
d. Business cycle

28. In economics, _____ is the use of government spending and revenue collection to influence the economy.

_____ can be contrasted with the other main type of economic policy, monetary policy, which attempts to stabilize the economy by controlling interest rates and the supply of money. The two main instruments of _____ are government spending and taxation.

a. Power III
b. Monetary policy
c. Tariff
d. Fiscal policy

29. _____ is the process by which the government, central bank (ii) availability of money, and (iii) cost of money or rate of interest, in order to attain a set of objectives oriented towards the growth and stability of the economy. Monetary theory provides insight into how to craft optimal _____.

Chapter 2. Determinants of Customer Behavior: Personal Factors and Market Environment

_____ is referred to as either being an expansionary policy where an expansionary policy increases the total supply of money in the economy, and a contractionary policy decreases the total money supply.

a. Fiscal policy
b. Tariff
c. Monetary policy
d. Power III

30. False advertising or _____ is the use of false or misleading statements in advertising. As advertising has the potential to persuade people into commercial transactions that they might otherwise avoid, many governments around the world use regulations to control false, deceptive or misleading advertising. Truth in labeling refers to essentially the same concept, that customers have the right to know what they are buying, and that all necessary information should be on the label.

a. Misleading advertising
b. Power III
c. Fine print
d. Deceptive advertising

31. The _____ is an independent agency of the United States government, established in 1914 by the _____ Act. Its principal mission is the promotion of 'consumer protection' and the elimination and prevention of what regulators perceive to be harmfully 'anti-competitive' business practices, such as coercive monopoly.

The _____ Act was one of President Wilson's major acts against trusts.

a. Power III
b. 180SearchAssistant
c. 6-3-5 Brainwriting
d. Federal Trade Commission

32. _____ is a form of communication that typically attempts to persuade potential customers to purchase or to consume more of a particular brand of product or service. 'While now central to the contemporary global economy and the reproduction of global production networks, it is only quite recently that _____ has been more than a marginal influence on patterns of sales and production. The formation of modern _____ was intimately bound up with the emergence of new forms of monopoly capitalism around the end of the 19th and beginning of the 20th century as one element in corporate strategies to create, organize and where possible control markets, especially for mass produced consumer goods.

Chapter 2. Determinants of Customer Behavior: Personal Factors and Market Environment

a. ACNielsen
b. ADTECH
c. AMAX
d. Advertising

33. The _____ is the primary federal law which governs occupational health and safety in the private sector and federal government in the United States. It was enacted by Congress in 1970 and was signed by President Richard Nixon on December 29, 1970. Its main goal is to ensure that employers provide employees with an environment free from recognized hazards, such as exposure to toxic chemicals, excessive noise levels, mechanical dangers, heat or cold stress, or unsanitary conditions.
   a. ACNielsen
   b. ADTECH
   c. AMAX
   d. Occupational Safety and Health Act

34. _____ is the ability of an individual or group to seclude themselves or information about themselves and thereby reveal themselves selectively. The boundaries and content of what is considered private differ among cultures and individuals, but share basic common themes. _____ is sometimes related to anonymity, the wish to remain unnoticed or unidentified in the public realm.
   a. 180SearchAssistant
   b. 6-3-5 Brainwriting
   c. Power III
   d. Privacy

35. The process of _____ involves the introduction of a good or service that is new or substantially improved. This includes, but is not limited to, improvements in functional characteristics, technical abilities, or ease of use.
   a. Product innovation
   b. Teaser rate
   c. Service-profit chain
   d. Discontinuation

36. _____ refers to the structured transmission of data between organizations by electronic means. It is used to transfer electronic documents from one computer system to another (ie) from one trading partner to another trading partner. It is more than mere E-mail; for instance, organizations might replace bills of lading and even checks with appropriate _____ messages.

Chapter 2. Determinants of Customer Behavior: Personal Factors and Market Environment

a. AMAX
b. ADTECH
c. ACNielsen
d. Electronic data interchange

37. _____ is a market coverage strategy in which a firm decides to ignore market segment differences and go after the whole market with one offer.it is type of marketing (or attempting to sell through persuasion) of a product to a wide audience. The idea is to broadcast a message that will reach the largest number of people possible. Traditionally _____ has focused on radio, television and newspapers as the medium used to reach this broad audience.

a. Cyberdoc
b. Business-to-consumer
c. Marketspace
d. Mass marketing

38. _____, in marketing, manufacturing, and management, is the use of flexible computer-aided manufacturing systems to produce custom output. Those systems combine the low unit costs of mass production processes with the flexibility of individual customization.

'_____' is the new frontier in business competition for both manufacturing and service industries.

a. Flanking marketing warfare strategies
b. Power III
c. Vertical integration
d. Mass customization

39. _____ is an advertisement in which a particular product specifically mentions a competitor by name for the express purpose of showing why the competitor is inferior to the product naming it.

This should not be confused with parody advertisements, where a fictional product is being advertised for the purpose of poking fun at the particular advertisement, nor should it be confused with the use of a coined brand name for the purpose of comparing the product without actually naming an actual competitor. ('Wikipedia tastes better and is less filling than the Encyclopedia Galactica.')

In the 1980s, during what has been referred to as the cola wars, soft-drink manufacturer Pepsi ran a series of advertisements where people, caught on hidden camera, in a blind taste test, chose Pepsi over rival Coca-Cola.

a. Cost per conversion
b. Comparative advertising
c. Heavy-up
d. GL-70

40. _____ refers generally to a strong enthusiasm for technology, especially new technologies such as personal computers, the Internet, mobile phones and home cinema. The term is used in sociology when examining the interaction of individuals with their society, especially contrasted with technophobia.

_____ and technophobia are the two extremes of the relationship between technology and society.

a. 180SearchAssistant
b. 6-3-5 Brainwriting
c. Power III
d. Technophilia

41. _____ is the fear or dislike of advanced technology or complex devices, especially computers. The term is generally used in the sense of an irrational fear, but others contend fears are justified. It is the opposite of technophilia.
a. 6-3-5 Brainwriting
b. Power III
c. Technophobia
d. 180SearchAssistant

42. On an intranet or B2E Enterprise Web portals, personalization is often based on user attributes such as department, functional area, or role. The term _____ in this context refers to the ability of users to modify the page layout or specify what content should be displayed.

There are two categories of personalizations:

1. Rule-based
2. Content-based

Web personalization models include rules-based filtering, based on 'if this, then that' rules processing, and collaborative filtering, which serves relevant material to customers by combining their own personal preferences with the preferences of like-minded others. Collaborative filtering works well for books, music, video, etc.

Chapter 2. Determinants of Customer Behavior: Personal Factors and Market Environment

a. Cashmere Agency
b. Self branding
c. Movin'
d. Customization

43. _____ refer to a collection of facts usually collected as the result of experience, observation or experiment or a set of premises. This may consist of numbers, words particularly as measurements or observations of a set of variables. _____ are often viewed as a lowest level of abstraction from which information and knowledge are derived.
   a. Sample size
   b. Mean
   c. Pearson product-moment correlation coefficient
   d. Data

44. _____ can be regarded as an outcome of mental processes (cognitive process) leading to the selection of a course of action among several alternatives. Every _____ process produces a final choice. The output can be an action or an opinion of choice.
   a. 180SearchAssistant
   b. 6-3-5 Brainwriting
   c. Power III
   d. Decision making

Chapter 3. Trends in Determinants of Customer Behavior

1. _____ is the study of when, why, how, where and what people do or do not buy products. It blends elements from psychology, sociology, social psychology, anthropology and economics. It attempts to understand the buyer decision making process, both individually and in groups. It studies characteristics of individual consumers such as demographics and behavioural variables in an attempt to understand people's wants. It also tries to assess influences on the consumer from groups such as family, friends, reference groups, and society in general.

    a. Communal marketing
    b. Consumer confidence
    c. Consumer behavior
    d. Multidimensional scaling

2. _____ or _____ data refers to selected population characteristics as used in government, marketing or opinion research, or the _____ profiles used in such research. Note the distinction from the term 'demography' Commonly-used _____ include race, age, income, disabilities, mobility (in terms of travel time to work or number of vehicles available), educational attainment, home ownership, employment status, and even location.

    a. African Americans
    b. AStore
    c. Albert Einstein
    d. Demographic

3. The _____ is a model used to represent the process of explaining the transformation of countries from high birth rates and high death rates to low birth rates and low death rates as part of the economic development of a country from a pre-industrial to an industrialized economy. It is based on an interpretation begun in 1929 by the American demographer Warren Thompson of prior observed changes, or transitions, in birth and death rates in industrialized societies over the past two hundred years.

    Most developed countries are beyond stage three of the model; the majority of developing countries are in stage 2 or stage 3.

    a. Power III
    b. 180SearchAssistant
    c. Demographic transition model
    d. 6-3-5 Brainwriting

4. Electronic commerce, commonly known as _____ or eCommerce, consists of the buying and selling of products or services over electronic systems such as the Internet and other computer networks. The amount of trade conducted electronically has grown extraordinarily with wide-spread Internet usage. A wide variety of commerce is conducted in this way, spurring and drawing on innovations in electronic funds transfer, supply chain management, Internet marketing, online transaction processing, electronic data interchange (EDI), inventory management systems, and automated data collection systems.

a. E-commerce
b. ACNielsen
c. AMAX
d. ADTECH

5. _____ is a modern day comedy of cross-cultural conflict and romance, directed by John Jeffcoat, released in 2006.

Todd Anderson (Josh Hamilton) spends his days managing a customer call center for Western Novelty, an American novelty product company, in Seattle, until he and his entire department are _____ to India. Adding insult to injury, Todd is sent to India to train his replacement.

a. ADTECH
b. ACNielsen
c. AMAX
d. Outsourced

6. _____ is the name given to the trend that sees individuals socializing less and retreating into their home more. Individuals tend to stay away from society and lack in social confidence leading to '_____'. The term was coined in the 1990s by Faith Popcorn a trend forecaster and marketing consultant.

a. Cocooning
b. Gruppi di Acquisto Solidale
c. Shopping Neutral
d. Diderot effect

7. An _____ is an unplanned or otherwise spontaneous purchase. One who tends to make such purchases is referred to as an impulse purchaser or impulse buyer.

Marketers and retailers tend to exploit these impulses which are tied to the basic want for instant gratification.

a. ACNielsen
b. Impulse purchase
c. AMAX
d. ADTECH

8. _____ or delayed gratification is the ability to wait in order to obtain something that one wants. This ability is usually considered to be a personality trait which is important for life success. Daniel Goleman has suggested that it is an important component of emotional intelligence.

a. Power III
b. 180SearchAssistant
c. Deferred gratification
d. 6-3-5 Brainwriting

9. In calculus, a function f defined on a subset of the real numbers with real values is called _____, if for all x and y such that x ≤ y one has f(x) ≤ f(y), so f preserves the order. In layman's terms, the sign of the slope is always positive (the curve tending upwards) or zero (i.e., non-decreasing, or asymptotic, or depicted as a horizontal, flat line) Likewise, a function is called monotonically decreasing (non-increasing) if, whenever x ≤ y, then f(x) ≥ f(y), so it reverses the order.

a. 6-3-5 Brainwriting
b. 180SearchAssistant
c. Power III
d. Monotonic

10. _____ in economics and business is the result of an exchange and from that trade we assign a numerical monetary value to a good, service or asset. If I trade 4 apples for an orange, the _____ of an orange is 4 - apples. Inversely, the _____ of an apple is 1/4 oranges.

a. Discounts and allowances
b. Price
c. Contribution margin-based pricing
d. Pricing

11. In descriptive statistics, the _____ is the length of the smallest interval which contains all the data. It is calculated by subtracting the smallest observation (sample minimum) from the greatest (sample maximum) and provides an indication of statistical dispersion.

It is measured in the same units as the data.

a. Range
b. Personalization
c. Just-In-Case
d. Japan Advertising Photographers' Association

12. _____ is the variety of human societies or cultures in a specific region, or in the world as a whole. (The term is also sometimes used to refer to multiculturalism within an organisation)

a. 6-3-5 Brainwriting
b. 180SearchAssistant
c. Cultural diversity
d. Power III

13. _____ is the study of the Earth and its lands, features, inhabitants, and phenomena. A literal translation would be 'to describe or write about the Earth'. The first person to use the word '_____' was Eratosthenes.
   a. 6-3-5 Brainwriting
   b. Geography
   c. Power III
   d. 180SearchAssistant

14. On an intranet or B2E Enterprise Web portals, personalization is often based on user attributes such as department, functional area, or role. The term _____ in this context refers to the ability of users to modify the page layout or specify what content should be displayed.

There are two categories of personalizations:

1. Rule-based
2. Content-based

Web personalization models include rules-based filtering, based on 'if this, then that' rules processing, and collaborative filtering, which serves relevant material to customers by combining their own personal preferences with the preferences of like-minded others. Collaborative filtering works well for books, music, video, etc.

   a. Self branding
   b. Cashmere Agency
   c. Movin'
   d. Customization

15. _____ is a market coverage strategy in which a firm decides to ignore market segment differences and go after the whole market with one offer. it is type of marketing (or attempting to sell through persuasion) of a product to a wide audience. The idea is to broadcast a message that will reach the largest number of people possible. Traditionally _____ has focused on radio, television and newspapers as the medium used to reach this broad audience.
   a. Cyberdoc
   b. Business-to-consumer
   c. Marketspace
   d. Mass marketing

Chapter 3. Trends in Determinants of Customer Behavior

16. _____, in marketing, manufacturing, and management, is the use of flexible computer-aided manufacturing systems to produce custom output. Those systems combine the low unit costs of mass production processes with the flexibility of individual customization.

'_____' is the new frontier in business competition for both manufacturing and service industries.

 a. Power III
 b. Flanking marketing warfare strategies
 c. Vertical integration
 d. Mass customization

17. In economics, _____ is the removal of intermediaries in a supply chain: 'cutting out the middleman'. Instead of going through traditional distribution channels, which had some type of intermediate (such as a distributor, wholesaler, broker, or agent), companies may now deal with every customer directly, for example via the Internet. One important factor is a drop in the cost of servicing customers directly.
 a. Disintermediation
 b. Spamvertising
 c. Consumer-to-consumer
 d. Social shopping

18. _____ is subcontracting a process, such as product design or manufacturing, to a third-party company. The decision to outsource is often made in the interest of lowering cost or making better use of time and energy costs, redirecting or conserving energy directed at the competencies of a particular business, or to make more efficient use of land, labor, capital, (information) technology and resources. _____ became part of the business lexicon during the 1980s.
 a. Outsourcing
 b. Intangible assets
 c. ACNielsen
 d. In-house

19. _____s is the social science that studies the production, distribution, and consumption of goods and services. The term _____s comes from the Ancient Greek oá¼°κονομῖα from oá¼¶κος (oikos, 'house') + vĭŒμος (nomos, 'custom' or 'law'), hence 'rules of the house(hold)'. Current _____ models developed out of the broader field of political economy in the late 19th century, owing to a desire to use an empirical approach more akin to the physical sciences.
 a. Industrial organization
 b. ADTECH
 c. Economic
 d. ACNielsen

20. _____ is a term used to describe how different aspects between economies are integrated. The basics of this theory were written by the Hungarian Economist Béla Balassa in the 1960s. As _____ increases, the barriers of trade between markets diminishes.
   a. ACNielsen
   b. ADTECH
   c. Incoterms
   d. Economic integration

21. _____ is a broad label that refers to any individuals or households that use goods and services generated within the economy. The concept of a _____ is used in different contexts, so that the usage and significance of the term may vary.

A _____ is a person who uses any product or service.

   a. Consumer
   b. 6-3-5 Brainwriting
   c. 180SearchAssistant
   d. Power III

22. _____ in organizations and public policy is both the organizational process of creating and maintaining a plan; and the psychological process of thinking about the activities required to create a desired goal on some scale. As such, it is a fundamental property of intelligent behavior. This thought process is essential to the creation and refinement of a plan, or integration of it with other plans, that is, it combines forecasting of developments with the preparation of scenarios of how to react to them.
   a. Power III
   b. 180SearchAssistant
   c. Planning
   d. 6-3-5 Brainwriting

23. _____ can be regarded as an outcome of mental processes (cognitive process) leading to the selection of a course of action among several alternatives. Every _____ process produces a final choice. The output can be an action or an opinion of choice.
   a. 180SearchAssistant
   b. 6-3-5 Brainwriting
   c. Power III
   d. Decision making

24. _____. People may not recognize the value in offered personalization, such as when firms offer to customize product offers. Many people don't want to receive any such offers, period.
   a. Push
   b. Bottling lines
   c. Category Development Index
   d. Little value placed on potential benefits

25. _____ is defined by the American _____ Association as the activity, set of institutions, and processes for creating, communicating, delivering, and exchanging offerings that have value for customers, clients, partners, and society at large. The term developed from the original meaning which referred literally to going to market, as in shopping, or going to a market to sell goods or services.

_____ practice tends to be seen as a creative industry, which includes advertising, distribution and selling.

   a. Marketing
   b. Customer acquisition management
   c. Marketing myopia
   d. Product naming

26. _____ is difficult to define. For example, in 1952, Alfred Kroeber and Clyde Kluckhohn compiled a list of 164 definitions of '_____' in _____: A Critical Review of Concepts and Definitions. However, the word '_____' is most commonly used in three basic senses:

   - excellence of taste in the fine arts and humanities
   - an integrated pattern of human knowledge, belief, and behavior that depends upon the capacity for symbolic thought and social learning
   - the set of shared attitudes, values, goals, and practices that characterizes an institution, organization or group.

When the concept first emerged in eighteenth- and nineteenth-century Europe, it connoted a process of cultivation or improvement, as in agriculture or horticulture. In the nineteenth century, it came to refer first to the betterment or refinement of the individual, especially through education, and then to the fulfillment of national aspirations or ideals.

   a. Albert Einstein
   b. AStore
   c. Culture
   d. African Americans

Chapter 4. The Customer as a Perceiver and Learner

1. In psychology, philosophy, and the cognitive sciences, _____ is the process of attaining awareness or understanding of sensory information. It is a task far more complex than was imagined in the 1950s and 1960s, when it was predicted that building perceiving machines would take about a decade, a goal which is still very far from fruition. The word _____ comes from the Latin words _____, percepio, meaning 'receiving, collecting, action of taking possession, apprehension with the mind or senses.'

_____ is one of the oldest fields in psychology.

   a. Groupthink
   b. Perception
   c. 180SearchAssistant
   d. Power III

2. _____ is a standard point of view or personal prejudice. especially when the tendency interferes with the ability to be impartial, unprejudiced, or objective. The term _____ed is used to describe an action, judgment, or other outcome influenced by a prejudged perspective.
   a. Bias
   b. Power III
   c. 6-3-5 Brainwriting
   d. 180SearchAssistant

3. In psychophysics, a _____, customarily abbreviated with lowercase letters as jnd, is the smallest detectable difference between a starting and secondary level of a particular sensory stimulus. It is also known as the difference limen or the differential threshold.

For many sensory modalities, over a wide range of stimulus magnitudes sufficiently far from the upper and lower limits of perception, the 'jnd' is a fixed proportion of the reference sensory level, and so the ratio of the jnd/reference is roughly constant (that is the jnd is a constant proportion/percentage of the reference level.)

   a. 180SearchAssistant
   b. Power III
   c. 6-3-5 Brainwriting
   d. Just noticeable difference

4. _____ in economics and business is the result of an exchange and from that trade we assign a numerical monetary value to a good, service or asset. If I trade 4 apples for an orange, the _____ of an orange is 4 - apples. Inversely, the _____ of an apple is 1/4 oranges.

a. Pricing
b. Contribution margin-based pricing
c. Discounts and allowances
d. Price

5. _____ is one of the four Ps of the marketing mix. The other three aspects are product, promotion, and place. It is also a key variable in microeconomic price allocation theory.
   a. Relationship based pricing
   b. Price
   c. Competitor indexing
   d. Pricing

6. A _____ refers to how a corporation is perceived. It is a generally accepted image of what a company 'stands for'. The creation of a _____ is an exercise in perception management.
   a. Lifetime value
   b. Demand generation
   c. Buying center
   d. Corporate image

7. A _____ is a collection of symbols, experiences and associations connected with a product, a service, a person or any other artifact or entity.

_____s have become increasingly important components of culture and the economy, now being described as 'cultural accessories and personal philosophies'.

Some people distinguish the psychological aspect of a _____ from the experiential aspect.

   a. Brand
   b. Store brand
   c. Brand equity
   d. Brandable software

8. Cognition is the scientific term for 'the process of thought.' Its usage varies in different ways in accord with different disciplines: For example, in psychology and _____ science it refers to an information processing view of an individual's psychological functions. Other interpretations of the meaning of cognition link it to the development of concepts; individual minds, groups, organizations, and even larger coalitions of entities, can be modelled as 'societies' (Society of Mind), which cooperate to form concepts.

Chapter 4. The Customer as a Perceiver and Learner

The autonomous elements of each 'society' would have the opportunity to demonstrate emergent behavior in the face of some crisis or opportunity.

a. Power III
b. 180SearchAssistant
c. Cognitive
d. 6-3-5 Brainwriting

9. _____ is a learning technique which avoids understanding of a subject and instead focuses on memorization. The major practice involved in _____ is learning by repetition. The idea is that one will be able to quickly recall the meaning of the material the more one repeats it.

a. 180SearchAssistant
b. 6-3-5 Brainwriting
c. Rote learning
d. Power III

10. _____ is a form of associative learning that was first demonstrated by Ivan Pavlov. The typical procedure for inducing _____ involves presentations of a neutral stimulus along with a stimulus of some significance. The neutral stimulus could be any event that does not result in an overt behavioral response from the organism under investigation. Pavlov referred to this as a conditioned stimulus (CS.)

a. 6-3-5 Brainwriting
b. 180SearchAssistant
c. Classical conditioning
d. Power III

11. _____ refers to a business or organization attempting to acquire goods or services to accomplish the goals of the enterprise. Though there are several organizations that attempt to set standards in the _____ process, processes can vary greatly between organizations. Typically the word '_____' is not used interchangeably with the word 'procurement', since procurement typically includes Expediting, Supplier Quality, and Traffic and Logistics (T'L) in addition to _____.

a. Supply network
b. Drop shipping
c. Supply chain
d. Purchasing

12. _____ is the process by which a new idea or new product is accepted by the market. The rate of _____ is the speed that the new idea spreads from one consumer to the next. Adoption is similar to _____ except that it deals with the psychological processes an individual goes through, rather than an aggregate market process.

a. Market development
b. Perceptual maps
c. Kano model
d. Diffusion

13. In probability theory, a branch of mathematics, a _____ is a solution to a stochastic differential equation. It is a continuous-time Markov process with continuous sample paths.

A sample path of a _____ mimics the trajectory of a molecule, which is embedded in a flowing fluid and at the same time subjected to random displacements due to collisions with other molecules, i.e. Brownian motion.

a. Diffusion process
b. 6-3-5 Brainwriting
c. Power III
d. 180SearchAssistant

14. _____ is a concept that arose out of the theory of two-step flow of communication propounded by Paul Lazarsfeld and Elihu Katz. This theory is one of several models that try to explain the diffusion of innovations, ideas, or commercial products.

The opinion leader is the agent who is an active media user and who interprets the meaning of media messages or content for lower-end media users.

a. Intellectual property
b. Elasticity
c. ACNielsen
d. Opinion leadership

15. _____ is a term developed by Eric von Hippel in 1986. His definition for _____ is:

1. _____s face needs that will be general in a marketplace - but face them months or years before the bulk of that marketplace encounters them, and
2. _____s are positioned to benefit significantly by obtaining a solution to those needs.

In other words: _____s are users of a product that currently experience needs still unknown to the public and who also benefit greatly if they obtain a solution to these needs.

Chapter 4. The Customer as a Perceiver and Learner

The _____ Method is a market research tool that may be used by companies and / or individuals seeking to develop breakthrough products. _____ methodology was originally developed by Dr. Eric von Hippel of the Massachusetts Institute of Technology (MIT) and first described in the July 1986 issue of the Journal of Management Science.

a. 6-3-5 Brainwriting
b. Power III
c. Lead user
d. 180SearchAssistant

16. _____ can be regarded as an outcome of mental processes (cognitive process) leading to the selection of a course of action among several alternatives. Every _____ process produces a final choice. The output can be an action or an opinion of choice.

a. 6-3-5 Brainwriting
b. Power III
c. Decision making
d. 180SearchAssistant

17. In environmental modeling and especially in hydrology, a _____ model means a model that is acceptably consistent with observed natural processes, i.e. that simulates well, for example, observed river discharge. It is a key concept of the so-called Generalized Likelihood Uncertainty Estimation (GLUE) methodology to quantify how uncertain environmental predictions are.

a. 180SearchAssistant
b. Power III
c. 6-3-5 Brainwriting
d. Behavioral

18. _____ is the subjective judgment that people make about the characteristics and severity of a risk. The phrase is most commonly used in reference to natural hazards and threats to the environment or health, such as nuclear power. Several theories have been proposed to explain why different people make different estimates of the dangerousness of risks.

a. Power III
b. 6-3-5 Brainwriting
c. 180SearchAssistant
d. Risk perception

19. In economics and related disciplines, a _____ is a cost incurred in making an economic exchange. For example, most people, when buying or selling a stock, must pay a commission to their broker; that commission is a _____ of doing the stock deal. Or consider buying a banana from a store; to purchase the banana, your costs will be not only the price of the banana itself, but also the energy and effort it requires to find out which of the various banana products you prefer, where to get them and at what price, the cost of traveling from your house to the store and back, the time waiting in line, and the effort of the paying itself; the costs above and beyond the cost of the banana are the _____s.
   a. Marginal cost
   b. Transaction cost
   c. Variable cost
   d. Fixed costs

20. A personal and cultural _____ is a relative ethic _____, an assumption upon which implementation can be extrapolated. A _____ system is a set of consistent _____s and measures that is soo not true. A principle _____ is a foundation upon which other _____s and measures of integrity are based.
   a. Package-on-Package
   b. Supreme Court of the United States
   c. Perceptual maps
   d. Value

21. _____, in marketing, consists of a consumer's commitment to repurchase the brand and can be demonstrated by repeated buying of a product or service or other positive behaviors such as word of mouth advocacy. True _____ implies that the consumer is willing, at least on occasion, to put aside their own desires in the interest of the brand. _____ has been proclaimed by some to be the ultimate goal of marketing.
   a. Brand implementation
   b. Trade Symbols
   c. Brand awareness
   d. Brand loyalty

22. In economics, business, retail, and accounting, a _____ is the value of money that has been used up to produce something, and hence is not available for use anymore. In economics, a _____ is an alternative that is given up as a result of a decision. In business, the _____ may be one of acquisition, in which case the amount of money expended to acquire it is counted as _____.
   a. Transaction cost
   b. Cost
   c. Variable cost
   d. Fixed costs

Chapter 4. The Customer as a Perceiver and Learner

23. _____ is difficult to define. For example, in 1952, Alfred Kroeber and Clyde Kluckhohn compiled a list of 164 definitions of '_____' in _____: A Critical Review of Concepts and Definitions. However, the word '_____' is most commonly used in three basic senses:

- excellence of taste in the fine arts and humanities
- an integrated pattern of human knowledge, belief, and behavior that depends upon the capacity for symbolic thought and social learning
- the set of shared attitudes, values, goals, and practices that characterizes an institution, organization or group.

When the concept first emerged in eighteenth- and nineteenth-century Europe, it connoted a process of cultivation or improvement, as in agriculture or horticulture. In the nineteenth century, it came to refer first to the betterment or refinement of the individual, especially through education, and then to the fulfillment of national aspirations or ideals.

   a. Culture
   b. Albert Einstein
   c. AStore
   d. African Americans

24. _____ is a concept that denotes the precise probability of specific eventualities. Technically, the notion of _____ is independent from the notion of value and, as such, eventualities may have both beneficial and adverse consequences. However, in general usage the convention is to focus only on potential negative impact to some characteristic of value that may arise from a future event.
   a. Power III
   b. 180SearchAssistant
   c. 6-3-5 Brainwriting
   d. Risk

25. _____ is the examining of goods or services from retailers with the intent to purchase at that time. _____ is an activity of selection and/or purchase. In some contexts it is considered a leisure activity as well as an economic one.
   a. Khodebshchik
   b. Shopping
   c. Hawkers
   d. Discount store

26. Electronic commerce, commonly known as _____ or eCommerce, consists of the buying and selling of products or services over electronic systems such as the Internet and other computer networks. The amount of trade conducted electronically has grown extraordinarily with wide-spread Internet usage. A wide variety of commerce is conducted in this way, spurring and drawing on innovations in electronic funds transfer, supply chain management, Internet marketing, online transaction processing, electronic data interchange (EDI), inventory management systems, and automated data collection systems.
   a. ACNielsen
   b. ADTECH
   c. AMAX
   d. E-commerce

Chapter 5. Customer Motivation: Needs, Emotions, and Psychographics

1. _____ is the set of reasons that determines one to engage in a particular behavior. The term is generally used for human _____ but, theoretically, it can be used to describe the causes for animal behavior as well
    a. Motivation
    b. 180SearchAssistant
    c. Role playing
    d. Power III

2. In the field of marketing, demographics, opinion research, and social research in general, _____ variables are any attributes relating to personality, values, attitudes, interests, or lifestyles. They are also called IAO variables. They can be contrasted with demographic variables (such as age and gender), behavioral variables (such as usage rate or loyalty), and bizographic variables (such as industry, seniority and functional area.)
    a. Business-to-business
    b. Marketing myopia
    c. Psychographic
    d. Lifetime value

3. _____s is the social science that studies the production, distribution, and consumption of goods and services. The term _____s comes from the Ancient Greek οἰκονομία from οἶκος (oikos, 'house') + νόμος (nomos, 'custom' or 'law'), hence 'rules of the house(hold)'. Current _____ models developed out of the broader field of political economy in the late 19th century, owing to a desire to use an empirical approach more akin to the physical sciences.
    a. Industrial organization
    b. Economic
    c. ACNielsen
    d. ADTECH

4. _____ is a term used to describe how different aspects between economies are integrated. The basics of this theory were written by the Hungarian Economist Béla Balassa in the 1960s. As _____ increases, the barriers of trade between markets diminishes.
    a. ADTECH
    b. Incoterms
    c. Economic integration
    d. ACNielsen

5. Maslow's _____ is a theory in psychology, proposed by Abraham Maslow in his 1943 paper A Theory of Human Motivation, which he subsequently extended to include his observations of humans' innate curiosity.

Maslow studied what he called exemplary people such as Albert Einstein, Jane Addams, Eleanor Roosevelt, and Frederick Douglass rather than mentally ill or neurotic people, writing that 'the study of crippled, stunted, immature, and unhealthy specimens can yield only a cripple psychology and a cripple philosophy.' Maslow also studied the healthiest one percent of the college student population. In his book, The Farther Reaches of Human Nature, Maslow writes, 'By ordinary standards of this kind of laboratory research...

a. Hierarchy of needs
b. 6-3-5 Brainwriting
c. Power III
d. 180SearchAssistant

6. _____ is defined by the American _____ Association as the activity, set of institutions, and processes for creating, communicating, delivering, and exchanging offerings that have value for customers, clients, partners, and society at large. The term developed from the original meaning which referred literally to going to market, as in shopping, or going to a market to sell goods or services.

_____ practice tends to be seen as a creative industry, which includes advertising, distribution and selling.

a. Product naming
b. Marketing
c. Customer acquisition management
d. Marketing myopia

7. The _____, in psychology, is a personality variable reflecting the extent to which people engage in and enjoy effortful cognitive activities.

People high in the _____ are more likely to form their attitudes by paying close attention to relevant arguments (i.e., via the central route to persuasion), whereas people low in the _____ are more likely to rely on peripheral cues, such as how attractive or credible a speaker is. Psychological research on the _____ has been conducted using self-report tests, where research participants answered a series of statements such as 'I prefer my life to be filled with puzzles that I must solve' and were scored on how much they felt the statements represented them.

a. Power III
b. Self-concept
c. 180SearchAssistant
d. Need for cognition

Chapter 5. Customer Motivation: Needs, Emotions, and Psychographics

8. In economics, an externality or spillover of an economic transaction is an impact on a party that is not directly involved in the transaction. In such a case, prices do not reflect the full costs or benefits in production or consumption of a product or service. A positive impact is called an _____ benefit, while a negative impact is called an _____ cost.
   a. External
   b. ACNielsen
   c. AMAX
   d. ADTECH

9. _____ is systematic determination of merit, worth, and significance of something or someone using criteria against a set of standards. _____ often is used to characterize and appraise subjects of interest in a wide range of human enterprises, including the arts, criminal justice, foundations and non-profit organizations, government, health care, and other human services.

Depending on the topic of interest, there are professional groups which look to the quality and rigor of the _____ process.

   a. AMAX
   b. ADTECH
   c. ACNielsen
   d. Evaluation

10. A personal and cultural _____ is a relative ethic _____, an assumption upon which implementation can be extrapolated. A _____ system is a set of consistent _____s and measures that is soo not true. A principle _____ is a foundation upon which other _____s and measures of integrity are based.
    a. Perceptual maps
    b. Value
    c. Package-on-Package
    d. Supreme Court of the United States

11. _____ is an investment technique that requires investors to purchase multiple financial products with different maturity dates.

_____ avoids the risk of reinvesting a big portion of assets in an unfavorable financial environment. For example, a person has both a 2015 matured CD and a 2018 matured CD.

a. 180SearchAssistant
b. Laddering
c. Power III
d. 6-3-5 Brainwriting

12. _____ or self identity refers to the global understanding a sentient being has of him or herself. It presupposes but can be distinguished from self-consciousness, which is simply an awareness of one's self. It is also more general than self-esteem, which is the purely evaluative element of the _____.

a. Self-concept
b. Need for cognition
c. 180SearchAssistant
d. Power III

13. _____ is the price at which an asset would trade in a competitive Walrasian auction setting. _____ is often used interchangeably with open _____, fair value or fair _____, although these terms have distinct definitions in different standards, and may differ in some circumstances.

International Valuation Standards defines _____ as 'the estimated amount for which a property should exchange on the date of valuation between a willing buyer and a willing seller in an arm's-length transaction after proper marketing wherein the parties had each acted knowledgeably, prudently, and without compulsion.'

_____ is a concept distinct from market price, which is 'the price at which one can transact', while _____ is 'the true underlying value' according to theoretical standards.

a. Power III
b. Restructuring
c. 180SearchAssistant
d. Market value

14. _____ was originally coined by Austrian psychologist Alfred Adler in 1929. The current broader sense of the word dates from 1961.

In sociology, a _____ is the way a person lives.

a. Power III
b. Lifestyle
c. 6-3-5 Brainwriting
d. 180SearchAssistant

Chapter 5. Customer Motivation: Needs, Emotions, and Psychographics   41

15. The acronym _____, is a psychographic segmentation. It was developed in the 1970s to explain changing U.S. values and lifestyles. It has since been reworked to enhance its ability to predict consumer behavior.

According to the _____ Framework, groups of people are arranged in a rectangle and are based on two dimensions. The vertical dimension segments people based on the degree to which they are innovative and have resources such as income, education, self-confidence, intelligence, leadership skills, and energy.

   a. 6-3-5 Brainwriting
   b. Power III
   c. 180SearchAssistant
   d. VALS

16. A _____ is a collection of symbols, experiences and associations connected with a product, a service, a person or any other artifact or entity.

_____s have become increasingly important components of culture and the economy, now being described as 'cultural accessories and personal philosophies'.

Some people distinguish the psychological aspect of a _____ from the experiential aspect.

   a. Brandable software
   b. Brand equity
   c. Store brand
   d. Brand

17. Human beings are also considered to be _____ because they have the ability to change raw materials into valuable _____. The term Human _____ can also be defined as the skills, energies, talents, abilities and knowledge that are used for the production of goods or the rendering of services. While taking into account human beings as _____, the following things have to be kept in mind:

   - The size of the population
   - The capabilities of the individuals in that population

Many _____ cannot be consumed in their original form. They have to be processed in order to change them into more usable commodities.

a. Resources
b. 6-3-5 Brainwriting
c. Power III
d. 180SearchAssistant

18. A _____ is a research instrument consisting of a series of questions and other prompts for the purpose of gathering information from respondents. Although they are often designed for statistical analysis of the responses, this is not always the case. The _____ was invented by Sir Francis Galton.
a. Mystery shopping
b. Mystery shoppers
c. Market research
d. Questionnaire

19. Oniomania is a medical term for the compulsive desire to shop. Oniomania is the technical term for the compulsive desire to shop, more commonly referred to as compulsive shopping, _____, shopping addiction or shopaholism. First described by Bleuler in 1915, and then Kraepelin in 1924, as oneomania from the Greek oneomai, to buy, included among other pathological and reactive impulses, _____ went largely ignored for nearly sixty years.
a. Trade credit
b. Retail loss prevention
c. Compulsive buying
d. Merchant

20. The philosophy of _____ holds that the only thing that exists is matter, and is considered a form of physicalism. Fundamentally, all things are composed of material and all phenomena (including consciousness) are the result of material interactions; therefore, matter is the only substance. As a theory, _____ belongs to the class of monist ontology.
a. Power III
b. 6-3-5 Brainwriting
c. 180SearchAssistant
d. Materialism

21. _____ is a lifestyle characterized by minimizing the 'more is better' pursuit of wealth and consumption. Adherents may choose _____ for a variety of personal reasons, such as spirituality, health, increase in 'quality time' for family and friends, stress reduction, personal taste or frugality. E. F. Schumacher put it best by saying, 'Any intelligent fool can make things bigger, more complex, and more violent.

a. Power III
b. Sustainable packaging
c. Simple living
d. Sustainable development

22. _____ can be regarded as an outcome of mental processes (cognitive process) leading to the selection of a course of action among several alternatives. Every _____ process produces a final choice. The output can be an action or an opinion of choice.
a. 180SearchAssistant
b. 6-3-5 Brainwriting
c. Power III
d. Decision making

Chapter 6. Customer Attitudes: Cognitive and Affective

1. Cognition is the scientific term for 'the process of thought.' Its usage varies in different ways in accord with different disciplines: For example, in psychology and _____ science it refers to an information processing view of an individual's psychological functions. Other interpretations of the meaning of cognition link it to the development of concepts; individual minds, groups, organizations, and even larger coalitions of entities, can be modelled as 'societies' (Society of Mind), which cooperate to form concepts.

   The autonomous elements of each 'society' would have the opportunity to demonstrate emergent behavior in the face of some crisis or opportunity.

   a. Cognitive
   b. 6-3-5 Brainwriting
   c. Power III
   d. 180SearchAssistant

2. Electronic commerce, commonly known as _____ or eCommerce, consists of the buying and selling of products or services over electronic systems such as the Internet and other computer networks. The amount of trade conducted electronically has grown extraordinarily with wide-spread Internet usage. A wide variety of commerce is conducted in this way, spurring and drawing on innovations in electronic funds transfer, supply chain management, Internet marketing, online transaction processing, electronic data interchange (EDI), inventory management systems, and automated data collection systems.
   a. E-commerce
   b. ADTECH
   c. AMAX
   d. ACNielsen

3. _____ is systematic determination of merit, worth, and significance of something or someone using criteria against a set of standards. _____ often is used to characterize and appraise subjects of interest in a wide range of human enterprises, including the arts, criminal justice, foundations and non-profit organizations, government, health care, and other human services.

   Depending on the topic of interest, there are professional groups which look to the quality and rigor of the _____ process.

   a. ACNielsen
   b. ADTECH
   c. AMAX
   d. Evaluation

4. A _____ is a collection of symbols, experiences and associations connected with a product, a service, a person or any other artifact or entity.

Chapter 6. Customer Attitudes: Cognitive and Affective

_____s have become increasingly important components of culture and the economy, now being described as 'cultural accessories and personal philosophies'.

Some people distinguish the psychological aspect of a _____ from the experiential aspect.

a. Store brand
b. Brand
c. Brandable software
d. Brand equity

5. _____ is the tendency to believe that one's own race or ethnic group is the most important and that some or all aspects of its culture are superior to those of other groups. Since within this ideology, individuals will judge other groups in relation to their own particular ethnic group or culture, especially with concern to language, behavior, customs, and religion. These ethnic distinctions and sub-divisions serve to define each ethnicity's unique cultural identity.
a. AStore
b. African Americans
c. Albert Einstein
d. Ethnocentrism

6. In economics and sociology, an _____ is any factor (financial or non-financial) that enables or motivates a particular course of action, or counts as a reason for preferring one choice to the alternatives. It is an expectation that encourages people to behave in a certain way. Since human beings are purposeful creatures, the study of _____ structures is central to the study of all economic activity (both in terms of individual decision-making and in terms of co-operation and competition within a larger institutional structure.)
a. ADTECH
b. AMAX
c. Incentive
d. ACNielsen

7. In psychology and education, a common definition of learning is a process that brings together cognitive, emotional, and environmental influences and experiences for acquiring, enhancing skills, values, and world views (Illeris,2000; Ormorod, 1995.) Learning as a process focuses on what happens when the learning takes place. Explanations of what happens constitute _____.

a. 180SearchAssistant
b. Self-concept
c. Learning theories
d. Power III

8. A _____ is a plan of action designed to achieve a particular goal. _____ is different from tactics. In military terms, tactics is concerned with the conduct of an engagement while _____ is concerned with how different engagements are linked.

   a. 180SearchAssistant
   b. Strategy
   c. Power III
   d. 6-3-5 Brainwriting

9. _____ is an uncomfortable feeling caused by holding two contradictory ideas simultaneously. The 'ideas' or 'cognitions' in question may include attitudes and beliefs, and also the awareness of one's behavior. The theory of _____ proposes that people have a motivational drive to reduce dissonance by changing their attitudes, beliefs, and behaviors, or by justifying or rationalizing their attitudes, beliefs, and behaviors.

   a. Power III
   b. Cognitive dissonance
   c. Perception
   d. 180SearchAssistant

10. The _____ is the social expectation that people will respond to each other in kind -- returning benefits for benefits, and responding with either indifference or hostility to harms. The social _____ often takes different forms in different areas of social life, or in different societies. All of them, however, are distinct from related ideas such as gratitude, the Golden Rule, or mutual goodwill.

    a. Classified magazine
    b. Driven media
    c. Norm of reciprocity
    d. Gambling advertising

11. In environmental modeling and especially in hydrology, a _____ model means a model that is acceptably consistent with observed natural processes, i.e. that simulates well, for example, observed river discharge. It is a key concept of the so-called Generalized Likelihood Uncertainty Estimation (GLUE) methodology to quantify how uncertain environmental predictions are.

    a. 180SearchAssistant
    b. 6-3-5 Brainwriting
    c. Behavioral
    d. Power III

Chapter 6. Customer Attitudes: Cognitive and Affective

12. _____, in marketing, consists of a consumer's commitment to repurchase the brand and can be demonstrated by repeated buying of a product or service or other positive behaviors such as word of mouth advocacy. True _____ implies that the consumer is willing, at least on occasion, to put aside their own desires in the interest of the brand. _____ has been proclaimed by some to be the ultimate goal of marketing.
    a. Brand implementation
    b. Brand awareness
    c. Trade Symbols
    d. Brand loyalty

13. A personal and cultural _____ is a relative ethic _____, an assumption upon which implementation can be extrapolated. A _____ system is a set of consistent _____s and measures that is soo not true. A principle _____ is a foundation upon which other _____s and measures of integrity are based.
    a. Value
    b. Perceptual maps
    c. Supreme Court of the United States
    d. Package-on-Package

14. A _____ is a list of the general tasks and responsibilities of a position. Typically, it also includes to whom the position reports, specifications such as the qualifications needed by the person in the job, salary range for the position, etc. A _____ is usually developed by conducting a job analysis, which includes examining the tasks and sequences of tasks necessary to perform the job.
    a. 6-3-5 Brainwriting
    b. Power III
    c. 180SearchAssistant
    d. Job description

15. _____ is the systematic application of marketing along with other concepts and techniques to achieve specific behavioral goals for a social good. _____ can be applied to promote, for example, merit goods, make the society avoid demerit goods and thus to promote that considers society's well being as a whole. This may include asking people not to smoke in public areas, for example, ask them to use seat belts, prompting to make them follow speed limits.
    a. Market development
    b. Marketing strategy
    c. Psychographic
    d. Social marketing

Chapter 6. Customer Attitudes: Cognitive and Affective

16. _____ is defined by the American _____ Association as the activity, set of institutions, and processes for creating, communicating, delivering, and exchanging offerings that have value for customers, clients, partners, and society at large. The term developed from the original meaning which referred literally to going to market, as in shopping, or going to a market to sell goods or services.

_____ practice tends to be seen as a creative industry, which includes advertising, distribution and selling.

a. Customer acquisition management
b. Marketing myopia
c. Product naming
d. Marketing

17. _____ can be regarded as an outcome of mental processes (cognitive process) leading to the selection of a course of action among several alternatives. Every _____ process produces a final choice. The output can be an action or an opinion of choice.
a. Power III
b. Decision making
c. 180SearchAssistant
d. 6-3-5 Brainwriting

Chapter 7. Researching Customer Behavior

1. _____ is the study of when, why, how, where and what people do or do not buy products. It blends elements from psychology, sociology, social psychology, anthropology and economics. It attempts to understand the buyer decision making process, both individually and in groups. It studies characteristics of individual consumers such as demographics and behavioural variables in an attempt to understand people's wants. It also tries to assess influences on the consumer from groups such as family, friends, reference groups, and society in general.
   a. Multidimensional scaling
   b. Communal marketing
   c. Consumer confidence
   d. Consumer behavior

2. _____ is difficult to define. For example, in 1952, Alfred Kroeber and Clyde Kluckhohn compiled a list of 164 definitions of '_____' in _____: A Critical Review of Concepts and Definitions. However, the word '_____' is most commonly used in three basic senses:

   - excellence of taste in the fine arts and humanities
   - an integrated pattern of human knowledge, belief, and behavior that depends upon the capacity for symbolic thought and social learning
   - the set of shared attitudes, values, goals, and practices that characterizes an institution, organization or group.

   When the concept first emerged in eighteenth- and nineteenth-century Europe, it connoted a process of cultivation or improvement, as in agriculture or horticulture. In the nineteenth century, it came to refer first to the betterment or refinement of the individual, especially through education, and then to the fulfillment of national aspirations or ideals.

   a. Albert Einstein
   b. African Americans
   c. AStore
   d. Culture

3. A personal and cultural _____ is a relative ethic _____, an assumption upon which implementation can be extrapolated. A _____ system is a set of consistent _____s and measures that is soo not true. A principle _____ is a foundation upon which other _____s and measures of integrity are based.
   a. Value
   b. Perceptual maps
   c. Supreme Court of the United States
   d. Package-on-Package

4. _____ is anything that is intended to save time, energy or frustration. A _____ store at a petrol station, for example, sells items that have nothing to do with gasoline/petrol, but it saves the consumer from having to go to a grocery store. '_____' is a very relative term and its meaning tends to change over time.

a. Demographic profile
b. Convenience
c. MaxDiff
d. Marketing buzz

5. _____ is a type of nonprobability sampling which involves the sample being drawn from that part of the population which is close to hand. That is, a sample population selected because it is readily available and convenient. The researcher using such a sample cannot scientifically make generalizations about the total population from this sample because it would not be representative enough.
   a. ADTECH
   b. ACNielsen
   c. Accidental sampling
   d. AMAX

6. A _____ is a form of qualitative research in which a group of people are asked about their attitude towards a product, service, concept, advertisement, idea, or packaging. Questions are asked in an interactive group setting where participants are free to talk with other group members.

Ernest Dichter originated the idea of having a 'group therapy' for products and this process is what became known as a _____.

   a. Marketing research process
   b. Logit analysis
   c. Cross tabulation
   d. Focus group

7. _____ is a field of inquiry that crosscuts disciplines and subject matters . _____ers aim to gather an in-depth understanding of human behavior and the reasons that govern such behavior. The discipline investigates the why and how of decision making, not just what, where, when.
   a. 6-3-5 Brainwriting
   b. 180SearchAssistant
   c. Qualitative research
   d. Power III

8. _____ is that part of statistical practice concerned with the selection of individual observations intended to yield some knowledge about a population of concern, especially for the purposes of statistical inference. Each observation measures one or more properties (weight, location, etc.) of an observable entity enumerated to distinguish objects or individuals.

a. Sampling
b. Richard Buckminster 'Bucky' Fuller
c. AStore
d. Sports Marketing Group

9. The _____ is an example of a projective test.

Historically, the _____ or _____ has been amongst the most widely used, researched, and taught projective psychological tests. Its adherents claim that it taps a subject's unconscious to reveal repressed aspects of personality, motives and needs for achievement, power and intimacy, and problem-solving abilities.

a. 6-3-5 Brainwriting
b. 180SearchAssistant
c. Power III
d. Thematic apperception test

10. _____ is a common word game involving an exchange of words that are associated together.

Once an original word has been chosen, usually randomly or arbitrarily, a player will find a word that they associate with it and make it known to all the players, usually by saying it aloud or writing it down as the next item on a list of words so far used. The next player must then do the same with this previous word.

a. Word association
b. Power III
c. 6-3-5 Brainwriting
d. 180SearchAssistant

11. _____ is a broad label that refers to any individuals or households that use goods and services generated within the economy. The concept of a _____ is used in different contexts, so that the usage and significance of the term may vary.

A _____ is a person who uses any product or service.

a. 180SearchAssistant
b. Consumer
c. 6-3-5 Brainwriting
d. Power III

Chapter 7. Researching Customer Behavior

12. _____ is the variety of human societies or cultures in a specific region, or in the world as a whole. (The term is also sometimes used to refer to multiculturalism within an organisation)
    a. 6-3-5 Brainwriting
    b. Power III
    c. 180SearchAssistant
    d. Cultural diversity

13. A _____ attribute is one that exists in a range of magnitudes, and can therefore be measured. Measurements of any particular _____ property are expressed as a specific quantity, referred to as a unit, multiplied by a number. Examples of physical quantities are distance, mass, and time.
    a. Quantitative
    b. Lifestyle city
    c. BeyondROI
    d. Dolly Dimples

14. A _____, in the field of business and marketing, is a geographic region or demographic group used to gauge the viability of a product or service in the mass market prior to a wide scale roll-out. The criteria used to judge the acceptability of a _____ region or group include:

    1. a population that is demographically similar to the proposed target market; and
    2. relative isolation from densely populated media markets so that advertising to the test audience can be efficient and economical.

The _____ ideally aims to duplicate 'everything' - promotion and distribution as well as `product' - on a smaller scale. The technique replicates, typically in one area, what is planned to occur in a national launch; and the results are very carefully monitored, so that they can be extrapolated to projected national results. The `area' may be any one of the following:

- Television area
- Test town
- Residential neighborhood
- Test site

A number of decisions have to be taken about any _____:

- Which _____?
- What is to be tested?
- How long a test?
- What are the success criteria?

The simple go or no-go decision, together with the related reduction of risk, is normally the main justification for the expense of _____s. At the same time, however, such _____s can be used to test specific elements of a new product's marketing mix; possibly the version of the product itself, the promotional message and media spend, the distribution channels and the price.

a. Power III
b. Test market
c. Preadolescence
d. 180SearchAssistant

15. _____ is defined by the American _____ Association as the activity, set of institutions, and processes for creating, communicating, delivering, and exchanging offerings that have value for customers, clients, partners, and society at large. The term developed from the original meaning which referred literally to going to market, as in shopping, or going to a market to sell goods or services.

_____ practice tends to be seen as a creative industry, which includes advertising, distribution and selling.

a. Marketing myopia
b. Customer acquisition management
c. Product naming
d. Marketing

16. _____ is the imitation of some real thing, state of affairs, or process. The act of simulating something generally entails representing certain key characteristics or behaviors of a selected physical or abstract system.

_____ is used in many contexts, including the modeling of natural systems or human systems in order to gain insight into their functioning.

a. 180SearchAssistant
b. 6-3-5 Brainwriting
c. Power III
d. Simulation

17. In environmental modeling and especially in hydrology, a _____ model means a model that is acceptably consistent with observed natural processes, i.e. that simulates well, for example, observed river discharge. It is a key concept of the so-called Generalized Likelihood Uncertainty Estimation (GLUE) methodology to quantify how uncertain environmental predictions are.

a. 6-3-5 Brainwriting
b. Power III
c. Behavioral
d. 180SearchAssistant

18. A _____ is a collection of symbols, experiences and associations connected with a product, a service, a person or any other artifact or entity.

_____s have become increasingly important components of culture and the economy, now being described as 'cultural accessories and personal philosophies'.

Some people distinguish the psychological aspect of a _____ from the experiential aspect.

a. Brandable software
b. Brand equity
c. Brand
d. Store brand

19. _____, in marketing, consists of a consumer's commitment to repurchase the brand and can be demonstrated by repeated buying of a product or service or other positive behaviors such as word of mouth advocacy. True _____ implies that the consumer is willing, at least on occasion, to put aside their own desires in the interest of the brand. _____ has been proclaimed by some to be the ultimate goal of marketing.
a. Trade Symbols
b. Brand implementation
c. Brand awareness
d. Brand loyalty

20. In psychology, philosophy, and the cognitive sciences, _____ is the process of attaining awareness or understanding of sensory information. It is a task far more complex than was imagined in the 1950s and 1960s, when it was predicted that building perceiving machines would take about a decade, a goal which is still very far from fruition. The word _____ comes from the Latin words _____, percepio, meaning 'receiving, collecting, action of taking possession, apprehension with the mind or senses.'

_____ is one of the oldest fields in psychology.

Chapter 7. Researching Customer Behavior 55

a. Groupthink
b. 180SearchAssistant
c. Power III
d. Perception

21. Perceptual mapping is a graphics technique used by asset marketers that attempts to visually display the perceptions of customers or potential customers. Typically the position of a product, product line, brand, or company is displayed relative to their competition.

_____ can have any number of dimensions but the most common is two dimensions.

a. Retail floor planning
b. Comparison-Shopping agent
c. Developed country
d. Perceptual maps

22. _____ psychogalvanic reflex is a method of measuring the electrical resistance of the skin. There has been a long history of electrodermal activity research, most of it dealing with spontaneous fluctuations. Most investigators accept the phenomenon without understanding exactly what it means.

a. Power III
b. 6-3-5 Brainwriting
c. 180SearchAssistant
d. Galvanic skin response

23. _____ involves the summary, collation and/or synthesis of existing research rather than primary research, where data is collected from, for example, research subjects or experiments.

The term is widely used in market research and in medical research. The principal methodology in medical _____ is the systematic review, commonly using meta-analytic statistical techniques, although other methods of synthesis, like realist reviews and meta-narrative reviews, have been developed in recent years.

a. Power III
b. 6-3-5 Brainwriting
c. Secondary research
d. 180SearchAssistant

Chapter 7. Researching Customer Behavior

24. _____ refer to a collection of facts usually collected as the result of experience, observation or experiment or a set of premises. This may consist of numbers, words particularly as measurements or observations of a set of variables. _____ are often viewed as a lowest level of abstraction from which information and knowledge are derived.
   a. Sample size
   b. Data
   c. Pearson product-moment correlation coefficient
   d. Mean

25. _____ is an advertisement in which a particular product specifically mentions a competitor by name for the express purpose of showing why the competitor is inferior to the product naming it.

This should not be confused with parody advertisements, where a fictional product is being advertised for the purpose of poking fun at the particular advertisement, nor should it be confused with the use of a coined brand name for the purpose of comparing the product without actually naming an actual competitor. ('Wikipedia tastes better and is less filling than the Encyclopedia Galactica.')

In the 1980s, during what has been referred to as the cola wars, soft-drink manufacturer Pepsi ran a series of advertisements where people, caught on hidden camera, in a blind taste test, chose Pepsi over rival Coca-Cola.

   a. Cost per conversion
   b. Heavy-up
   c. GL-70
   d. Comparative advertising

26. A _____ is a structured collection of records or data that is stored in a computer system. The structure is achieved by organizing the data according to a _____ model. The model in most common use today is the relational model.
   a. Power III
   b. Database
   c. 6-3-5 Brainwriting
   d. 180SearchAssistant

27. _____ is a term used to describe a process of preparing and collecting data - for example as part of a process improvement or similar project.

Chapter 7. Researching Customer Behavior

_____ usually takes place early on in an improvement project, and is often formalised through a _____ Plan which often contains the following activity.

1. Pre collection activity - Agree goals, target data, definitions, methods
2. Collection - _____
3. Present Findings - usually involves some form of sorting analysis and/or presentation.

A formal _____ process is necessary as it ensures that data gathered is both defined and accurate and that subsequent decisions based on arguments embodied in the findings are valid . The process provides both a baseline from which to measure from and in certain cases a target on what to improve. Types of _____ 1-By mail questionnaires 2-By personal interview

- Six sigma
- Sampling (statistics)

a. 6-3-5 Brainwriting
b. Power III
c. Data collection
d. 180SearchAssistant

28. _____ is a technology which allows a user to interact with a computer-simulated environment, whether that environment is a simulation of the real world or an imaginary world. Most current _____ environments are primarily visual experiences, displayed either on a computer screen or through special or stereoscopic displays, but some simulations include additional sensory information, such as sound through speakers or headphones. Some advanced, haptic systems now include tactile information, generally known as force feedback, in medical and gaming applications.
   a. Power III
   b. Virtual reality
   c. 180SearchAssistant
   d. 6-3-5 Brainwriting

29. _____ is the examining of goods or services from retailers with the intent to purchase at that time. _____ is an activity of selection and/or purchase. In some contexts it is considered a leisure activity as well as an economic one.
   a. Khodebshchik
   b. Hawkers
   c. Discount store
   d. Shopping

Chapter 7. Researching Customer Behavior

30. Electronic commerce, commonly known as _____ or eCommerce, consists of the buying and selling of products or services over electronic systems such as the Internet and other computer networks. The amount of trade conducted electronically has grown extraordinarily with wide-spread Internet usage. A wide variety of commerce is conducted in this way, spurring and drawing on innovations in electronic funds transfer, supply chain management, Internet marketing, online transaction processing, electronic data interchange (EDI), inventory management systems, and automated data collection systems.
   a. ADTECH
   b. E-commerce
   c. AMAX
   d. ACNielsen

31. _____ can be regarded as an outcome of mental processes (cognitive process) leading to the selection of a course of action among several alternatives. Every _____ process produces a final choice. The output can be an action or an opinion of choice.
   a. 6-3-5 Brainwriting
   b. 180SearchAssistant
   c. Power III
   d. Decision making

Chapter 8. Individual Customer Decision Making

1. _____ can be regarded as an outcome of mental processes (cognitive process) leading to the selection of a course of action among several alternatives. Every _____ process produces a final choice. The output can be an action or an opinion of choice.
   a. 6-3-5 Brainwriting
   b. Power III
   c. Decision making
   d. 180SearchAssistant

2. In economics, business, retail, and accounting, a _____ is the value of money that has been used up to produce something, and hence is not available for use anymore. In economics, a _____ is an alternative that is given up as a result of a decision. In business, the _____ may be one of acquisition, in which case the amount of money expended to acquire it is counted as _____.
   a. Fixed costs
   b. Variable cost
   c. Transaction cost
   d. Cost

3. _____ generally refers to a list of all planned expenses and revenues. It is a plan for saving and spending. A _____ is an important concept in microeconomics, which uses a _____ line to illustrate the trade-offs between two or more goods.
   a. 180SearchAssistant
   b. Power III
   c. Budget
   d. 6-3-5 Brainwriting

4. _____ is the study of when, why, how, where and what people do or do not buy products. It blends elements from psychology, sociology,social psychology, anthropology and economics. It attempts to understand the buyer decision making process, both individually and in groups. It studies characteristics of individual consumers such as demographics and behavioural variables in an attempt to understand people's wants. It also tries to assess influences on the consumer from groups such as family, friends, reference groups, and society in general.
   a. Multidimensional scaling
   b. Consumer confidence
   c. Communal marketing
   d. Consumer behavior

5. In economics, an externality or spillover of an economic transaction is an impact on a party that is not directly involved in the transaction. In such a case, prices do not reflect the full costs or benefits in production or consumption of a product or service. A positive impact is called an _____ benefit, while a negative impact is called an _____ cost.

Chapter 8. Individual Customer Decision Making

   a. AMAX
   b. ADTECH
   c. ACNielsen
   d. External

6. In economics, _____ is the desire to own something and the ability to pay for it. The term _____ signifies the ability or the willingness to buy a particular commodity at a given point of time .

   a. Market system
   b. Demand
   c. Market dominance
   d. Discretionary spending

7. _____ commonly refers to the electronic retailing / _____ channels industry, which includes such billion dollar companies as Home shoppingN, QVC, eBay, ShopNBC, Buy.com, and Amazon.com. _____ allows consumers to shop for goods while in the privacy of their own home, as opposed to traditional shopping, which requires you to visit brick and mortar stores and shopping malls.

The _____ / electronic retailing industry was created in 1977 when small market radio talk show host Bob Circosta was asked to sell avocado-green-colored can openers live on the air by station owner Bud Paxson when an advertiser traded 112 units of product instead of paying his advertising bill.

   a. 180SearchAssistant
   b. Home Shopping
   c. 6-3-5 Brainwriting
   d. Power III

8. _____ is the examining of goods or services from retailers with the intent to purchase at that time. _____ is an activity of selection and/or purchase. In some contexts it is considered a leisure activity as well as an economic one.
   a. Hawkers
   b. Discount store
   c. Khodebshchik
   d. Shopping

9. A _____ is a plan of action designed to achieve a particular goal.

Chapter 8. Individual Customer Decision Making

_____ is different from tactics. In military terms, tactics is concerned with the conduct of an engagement while _____ is concerned with how different engagements are linked.

a. 180SearchAssistant
b. Power III
c. 6-3-5 Brainwriting
d. Strategy

10. _____ is the subjective judgment that people make about the characteristics and severity of a risk. The phrase is most commonly used in reference to natural hazards and threats to the environment or health, such as nuclear power. Several theories have been proposed to explain why different people make different estimates of the dangerousness of risks.

a. Power III
b. 6-3-5 Brainwriting
c. Risk perception
d. 180SearchAssistant

11. In algebra, a _____ is a function depending on n that associates a scalar, det(A), to an n×n square matrix A. The fundamental geometric meaning of a _____ is a scale factor for measure when A is regarded as a linear transformation. _____s are important both in calculus, where they enter the substitution rule for several variables, and in multilinear algebra.

For a fixed nonnegative integer n, there is a unique _____ function for the n×n matrices over any commutative ring R. In particular, this function exists when R is the field of real or complex numbers.

a. Black Friday
b. Motion Picture Association of America's film-rating system
c. Package-on-Package
d. Determinant

12. _____ is a concept that denotes the precise probability of specific eventualities. Technically, the notion of _____ is independent from the notion of value and, as such, eventualities may have both beneficial and adverse consequences. However, in general usage the convention is to focus only on potential negative impact to some characteristic of value that may arise from a future event.

a. 6-3-5 Brainwriting
b. Risk
c. Power III
d. 180SearchAssistant

13. _____ is a broad label that refers to any individuals or households that use goods and services generated within the economy. The concept of a _____ is used in different contexts, so that the usage and significance of the term may vary.

A _____ is a person who uses any product or service.

a. 180SearchAssistant
b. Power III
c. Consumer
d. 6-3-5 Brainwriting

14. A _____ is a collection of symbols, experiences and associations connected with a product, a service, a person or any other artifact or entity.

_____s have become increasingly important components of culture and the economy, now being described as 'cultural accessories and personal philosophies'.

Some people distinguish the psychological aspect of a _____ from the experiential aspect.

a. Store brand
b. Brand
c. Brandable software
d. Brand equity

15. _____ is a slang term for a newcomer to an Internet activity, for example online gaming. It can also be used for any other activity in whose context a somewhat clueless newcomer could exist. It can have derogatory connotations, but is also often used for descriptive purposes only, without a value judgment.

a. 6-3-5 Brainwriting
b. Power III
c. 180SearchAssistant
d. Newbie

Chapter 8. Individual Customer Decision Making

16. _____ is difficult to define. For example, in 1952, Alfred Kroeber and Clyde Kluckhohn compiled a list of 164 definitions of '_____' in _____: A Critical Review of Concepts and Definitions. However, the word '_____' is most commonly used in three basic senses:

- excellence of taste in the fine arts and humanities
- an integrated pattern of human knowledge, belief, and behavior that depends upon the capacity for symbolic thought and social learning
- the set of shared attitudes, values, goals, and practices that characterizes an institution, organization or group.

When the concept first emerged in eighteenth- and nineteenth-century Europe, it connoted a process of cultivation or improvement, as in agriculture or horticulture. In the nineteenth century, it came to refer first to the betterment or refinement of the individual, especially through education, and then to the fulfillment of national aspirations or ideals.

a. Albert Einstein
b. AStore
c. Culture
d. African Americans

17. _____ is an advertisement in which a particular product specifically mentions a competitor by name for the express purpose of showing why the competitor is inferior to the product naming it.

This should not be confused with parody advertisements, where a fictional product is being advertised for the purpose of poking fun at the particular advertisement, nor should it be confused with the use of a coined brand name for the purpose of comparing the product without actually naming an actual competitor. ('Wikipedia tastes better and is less filling than the Encyclopedia Galactica.')

In the 1980s, during what has been referred to as the cola wars, soft-drink manufacturer Pepsi ran a series of advertisements where people, caught on hidden camera, in a blind taste test, chose Pepsi over rival Coca-Cola.

a. Comparative advertising
b. GL-70
c. Heavy-up
d. Cost per conversion

18. _____ is systematic determination of merit, worth, and significance of something or someone using criteria against a set of standards. _____ often is used to characterize and appraise subjects of interest in a wide range of human enterprises, including the arts, criminal justice, foundations and non-profit organizations, government, health care, and other human services.

Depending on the topic of interest, there are professional groups which look to the quality and rigor of the _____ process.

a. ACNielsen
b. Evaluation
c. AMAX
d. ADTECH

19. In grammar, the _____ is the form of an adjective or adverb which denotes the degree or grade by which a person, thing and is used in this context with a subordinating conjunction, such as than, as...as, etc.

The structure of a _____ in English consists normally of the positive form of the adjective or adverb, plus the suffix -er e.g. 'he is taller than his father is', or 'the village is less picturesque than the town nearby'.

a. Power III
b. 6-3-5 Brainwriting
c. Comparative
d. 180SearchAssistant

20. _____ is the realization of an application idea, model, design, specification, standard, algorithm an _____ is a realization of a technical specification or algorithm as a program, software component, or other computer system. Many _____s may exist for a given specification or standard.

a. AMAX
b. ADTECH
c. Implementation
d. ACNielsen

Chapter 9. Institution Customer Decision Making: Household, Business, and Government

1. _____ can be regarded as an outcome of mental processes (cognitive process) leading to the selection of a course of action among several alternatives. Every _____ process produces a final choice. The output can be an action or an opinion of choice.
   a. Power III
   b. 6-3-5 Brainwriting
   c. Decision making
   d. 180SearchAssistant

2. _____ is a contract between two parties, one being the employer and the other being the employee. An employee may be defined as: 'A person in the service of another under any contract of hire, express or implied, oral or written, where the employer has the power or right to control and direct the employee in the material details of how the work is to be performed.' Black's Law Dictionary page 471 (5th ed. 1979.)
   a. ADTECH
   b. ACNielsen
   c. AMAX
   d. Employment

3. _____ is a broad label that refers to any individuals or households that use goods and services generated within the economy. The concept of a _____ is used in different contexts, so that the usage and significance of the term may vary.

   A _____ is a person who uses any product or service.

   a. Consumer
   b. 180SearchAssistant
   c. Power III
   d. 6-3-5 Brainwriting

4. _____ is the subjective judgment that people make about the characteristics and severity of a risk. The phrase is most commonly used in reference to natural hazards and threats to the environment or health, such as nuclear power. Several theories have been proposed to explain why different people make different estimates of the dangerousness of risks.
   a. Risk perception
   b. 6-3-5 Brainwriting
   c. Power III
   d. 180SearchAssistant

Chapter 9. Institution Customer Decision Making: Household, Business, and Government

5. _____ is a concept that denotes the precise probability of specific eventualities. Technically, the notion of _____ is independent from the notion of value and, as such, eventualities may have both beneficial and adverse consequences. However, in general usage the convention is to focus only on potential negative impact to some characteristic of value that may arise from a future event.

   a. 6-3-5 Brainwriting
   b. Risk
   c. Power III
   d. 180SearchAssistant

6. _____ can be defined that the kind of relationship you have with your business. The main three basic business organizational structures are sole proprietorships, partnerships and corporations.

A sole proprietorship is the most common and easiest way to create your own business. Generally, anyone who performs services of any kind, such as a server, caterer is by default a sole proprietor unless he or she takes specific action to set it up other-wise. Any small company with only one employee is often kept as a sole proprietorship, but there are no restrictions that how big a sole proprietorship can become.

   a. Door-to-door
   b. Business structure
   c. Marketing management
   d. Fast moving consumer goods

7. Human beings are also considered to be _____ because they have the ability to change raw materials into valuable _____. The term Human _____ can also be defined as the skills, energies, talents, abilities and knowledge that are used for the production of goods or the rendering of services. While taking into account human beings as _____, the following things have to be kept in mind:

   - The size of the population
   - The capabilities of the individuals in that population

Many _____ cannot be consumed in their original form. They have to be processed in order to change them into more usable commodities.

   a. Resources
   b. 180SearchAssistant
   c. Power III
   d. 6-3-5 Brainwriting

Chapter 9. Institution Customer Decision Making: Household, Business, and Government

8. A _____, in marketing, procurement, and organizational studies, is a group of employees, family members, or members of any type of organization responsible for purchasing an item for the organization. In a business setting, major purchases typically require input from various parts of the organization, including finance, accounting, purchasing, information technology management, and senior management. Highly technical purchases, such as information systems or production equipment, also require the expertise of technical specialists.

   a. Commercialization
   b. Marketing myopia
   c. Packshot
   d. Buying center

9. In economic models, the _____ time frame assumes no fixed factors of production. Firms can enter or leave the marketplace, and the cost (and availability) of land, labor, raw materials, and capital goods can be assumed to vary. In contrast, in the short-run time frame, certain factors are assumed to be fixed, because there is not sufficient time for them to change.

   a. 6-3-5 Brainwriting
   b. Long-run
   c. 180SearchAssistant
   d. Power III

10. In economics, business, retail, and accounting, a _____ is the value of money that has been used up to produce something, and hence is not available for use anymore. In economics, a _____ is an alternative that is given up as a result of a decision. In business, the _____ may be one of acquisition, in which case the amount of money expended to acquire it is counted as _____.

    a. Variable cost
    b. Fixed costs
    c. Transaction cost
    d. Cost

11. _____ is a form of social influence. It is the process of guiding people toward the adoption of an idea, attitude, or action by rational and symbolic (though not always logical) means. It is strategy of problem-solving relying on 'appeals' rather than coercion.

    a. Power III
    b. 180SearchAssistant
    c. 6-3-5 Brainwriting
    d. Persuasion

Chapter 9. Institution Customer Decision Making: Household, Business, and Government

12. _____ is the study of when, why, how, where and what people do or do not buy products. It blends elements from psychology, sociology, social psychology, anthropology and economics. It attempts to understand the buyer decision making process, both individually and in groups. It studies characteristics of individual consumers such as demographics and behavioural variables in an attempt to understand people's wants. It also tries to assess influences on the consumer from groups such as family, friends, reference groups, and society in general.
    a. Consumer behavior
    b. Communal marketing
    c. Multidimensional scaling
    d. Consumer confidence

13. Competitiveness is a comparative concept of the ability and performance of a firm, sub-sector or country to sell and supply goods and/or services in a given market. Although widely used in economics and business management, the usefulness of the concept, particularly in the context of national competitiveness, is vigorously disputed by economists, such as Paul Krugman.

    The term may also be applied to markets, where it is used to refer to the extent to which the market structure may be regarded as perfectly _____.

    a. Geographical pricing
    b. Customs union
    c. Free trade zone
    d. Competitive

14. _____ refers to 'controlling human or societal behaviour by rules or restrictions.' _____ can take many forms: legal restrictions promulgated by a government authority, self-_____, social _____, co-_____ and market _____. One can consider _____ as actions of conduct imposing sanctions (such as a fine.) This action of administrative law, or implementing regulatory law, may be contrasted with statutory or case law.
    a. CAN-SPAM
    b. Rule of four
    c. Non-conventional trademark
    d. Regulation

15. A _____ is an invitation for suppliers, often through a bidding process, to submit a proposal on a specific commodity or service. A bidding process is one of the best methods for leveraging a company's negotiating ability and purchasing power with suppliers. The _____ process brings structure to the procurement decision and allows the risks and benefits to be identified clearly upfront.

Chapter 9. Institution Customer Decision Making: Household, Business, and Government

a. Request for proposal
b. Hit rate
c. Lead generation
d. Sales management

16. A _____ is an explicit set of requirements to be satisfied by a material, product, or service.

In engineering, manufacturing, and business, it is vital for suppliers, purchasers, and users of materials, products, or services to understand and agree upon all requirements. A _____ is a type of a standard which is often referenced by a contract or procurement document.

a. Product optimization
b. Specification
c. Product development
d. New product development

17. _____ is one of the four Ps of the marketing mix. The other three aspects are product, promotion, and place. It is also a key variable in microeconomic price allocation theory.
a. Relationship based pricing
b. Price
c. Competitor indexing
d. Pricing

18. _____ refers to a business or organization attempting to acquire goods or services to accomplish the goals of the enterprise. Though there are several organizations that attempt to set standards in the _____ process, processes can vary greatly between organizations. Typically the word '_____' is not used interchangeably with the word 'procurement', since procurement typically includes Expediting, Supplier Quality, and Traffic and Logistics (T'L) in addition to _____.
a. Drop shipping
b. Supply chain
c. Supply network
d. Purchasing

19. _____ is an advertisement in which a particular product specifically mentions a competitor by name for the express purpose of showing why the competitor is inferior to the product naming it.

Chapter 9. Institution Customer Decision Making: Household, Business, and Government

This should not be confused with parody advertisements, where a fictional product is being advertised for the purpose of poking fun at the particular advertisement, nor should it be confused with the use of a coined brand name for the purpose of comparing the product without actually naming an actual competitor. ('Wikipedia tastes better and is less filling than the Encyclopedia Galactica.')

In the 1980s, during what has been referred to as the cola wars, soft-drink manufacturer Pepsi ran a series of advertisements where people, caught on hidden camera, in a blind taste test, chose Pepsi over rival Coca-Cola.

a. Comparative advertising
b. Heavy-up
c. GL-70
d. Cost per conversion

20. In mathematics, an _____, or central tendency of a data set refers to a measure of the 'middle' or 'expected' value of the data set. There are many different descriptive statistics that can be chosen as a measurement of the central tendency of the data items.

An _____ is a single value that is meant to typify a list of values.

a. ACNielsen
b. AMAX
c. ADTECH
d. Average

21. _____ is the process by which a new idea or new product is accepted by the market. The rate of _____ is the speed that the new idea spreads from one consumer to the next. Adoption is similar to _____ except that it deals with the psychological processes an individual goes through, rather than an aggregate market process.

a. Diffusion
b. Perceptual maps
c. Market development
d. Kano model

22. _____ is the corporate management term for the act of partially dismantling or otherwise reorganizing a company for the purpose of making it more profitable. Also known as corporate _____, debt _____ and financial _____.

_____ is often done as part of a bankruptcy or of a strategic takeover by another firm, such as a leveraged buyout by a private equity firm.

a. 180SearchAssistant
b. Power III
c. Market value
d. Restructuring

23. A _____ is a relatively new executive level position at a corporation, company, organization typically reporting directly to the CEO or board of directors. The _____ is responsible for a brand's image, experience, and promise, and propagating it throughout all aspects of the company. The brand officer oversees marketing, advertising, design, public relations and customer service departments.
    a. Chief executive officer
    b. Financial analyst
    c. Power III
    d. Chief brand officer

24. _____s is the social science that studies the production, distribution, and consumption of goods and services. The term _____s comes from the Ancient Greek οἰκονομία from οἶκος (oikos, 'house') + νόμος (nomos, 'custom' or 'law'), hence 'rules of the house(hold)'. Current _____ models developed out of the broader field of political economy in the late 19th century, owing to a desire to use an empirical approach more akin to the physical sciences.
    a. ADTECH
    b. Economic
    c. Industrial organization
    d. ACNielsen

25. _____ is a term used to describe how different aspects between economies are integrated. The basics of this theory were written by the Hungarian Economist Béla Balassa in the 1960s. As _____ increases, the barriers of trade between markets diminishes.
    a. Economic integration
    b. ACNielsen
    c. ADTECH
    d. Incoterms

26. _____ in its literal sense is the process of transformation of local or regional phenomena into global ones. It can be described as a process by which the people of the world are unified into a single society and function together.

This process is a combination of economic, technological, sociocultural and political forces.

Chapter 9. Institution Customer Decision Making: Household, Business, and Government

a. 6-3-5 Brainwriting
b. Globalization
c. Power III
d. 180SearchAssistant

Chapter 10. Relationship-Based Buying

1. A supply chain is the system of organizations, people, technology, activities, information and resources involved in moving a product or service from _____ to customer. Supply chain activities transform natural resources, raw materials and components into a finished product that is delivered to the end customer. In sophisticated supply chain systems, used products may re-enter the supply chain at any point where residual value is recyclable.
   a. Bringin' Home the Oil
   b. Rebate
   c. Product line extension
   d. Supplier

2. _____ is the set of reasons that determines one to engage in a particular behavior. The term is generally used for human _____ but, theoretically, it can be used to describe the causes for animal behavior as well
   a. Role playing
   b. 180SearchAssistant
   c. Power III
   d. Motivation

3. _____ is the subjective judgment that people make about the characteristics and severity of a risk. The phrase is most commonly used in reference to natural hazards and threats to the environment or health, such as nuclear power. Several theories have been proposed to explain why different people make different estimates of the dangerousness of risks.
   a. Power III
   b. 180SearchAssistant
   c. 6-3-5 Brainwriting
   d. Risk perception

4. Switching barriers or _____s are terms used in microeconomics, strategic management, and marketing to describe any impediment to a customer's changing of suppliers.

   In many markets, consumers are forced to incur costs when switching from one supplier to another. These costs are called _____s and can come in many different shapes.

   a. Strategic business unit
   b. Strategic group
   c. Chaotics
   d. Switching cost

Chapter 10. Relationship-Based Buying

5. In economics, business, retail, and accounting, a _____ is the value of money that has been used up to produce something, and hence is not available for use anymore. In economics, a _____ is an alternative that is given up as a result of a decision. In business, the _____ may be one of acquisition, in which case the amount of money expended to acquire it is counted as _____.
   a. Fixed costs
   b. Variable cost
   c. Transaction cost
   d. Cost

6. _____ is a concept that denotes the precise probability of specific eventualities. Technically, the notion of _____ is independent from the notion of value and, as such, eventualities may have both beneficial and adverse consequences. However, in general usage the convention is to focus only on potential negative impact to some characteristic of value that may arise from a future event.
   a. Power III
   b. 6-3-5 Brainwriting
   c. 180SearchAssistant
   d. Risk

7. _____ refers to the additional value of a commodity over the cost of commodities used to produce it from the previous stage of production. An example is the price of gasoline at the pump over the price of the oil in it. In national accounts used in macroeconomics, it refers to the contribution of the factors of production, i.e., land, labor, and capital goods, to raising the value of a product and corresponds to the incomes received by the owners of these factors. The factors of production provide 'services' which raise the unit price of a product (X) relative to the cost per unit of intermediate goods used up in the production of X. _____ is shared between the factors of production (capital, labor, also human capital), giving rise to issues of distribution.
   a. Consumer spending
   b. Deregulation
   c. Power III
   d. Value added

8.

The net present value (NPV) of all of a company's customers in terms of customer loyalty and indirectly, the revenue that the company can obtain from them.

In deciding the value of a company, it is important to know of how much value its customer base is in terms of future revenues. The greater the _____ , the more future revenue in the lifetime of its clients; this means that a company with a higher _____ can get more money from its customers on average than another company that is identical in all other characteristics.

a. Total cost
b. Marginal revenue
c. Product proliferation
d. Customer equity

9. _____ is defined by the American _____ Association as the activity, set of institutions, and processes for creating, communicating, delivering, and exchanging offerings that have value for customers, clients, partners, and society at large. The term developed from the original meaning which referred literally to going to market, as in shopping, or going to a market to sell goods or services.

_____ practice tends to be seen as a creative industry, which includes advertising, distribution and selling.

a. Product naming
b. Marketing myopia
c. Customer acquisition management
d. Marketing

10. _____ refers to a business or organization attempting to acquire goods or services to accomplish the goals of the enterprise. Though there are several organizations that attempt to set standards in the _____ process, processes can vary greatly between organizations. Typically the word '_____' is not used interchangeably with the word 'procurement', since procurement typically includes Expediting, Supplier Quality, and Traffic and Logistics (T'L) in addition to _____.

a. Drop shipping
b. Supply chain
c. Supply network
d. Purchasing

11. In algebra, a _____ is a function depending on n that associates a scalar, det(A), to an n×n square matrix A. The fundamental geometric meaning of a _____ is a scale factor for measure when A is regarded as a linear transformation. _____s are important both in calculus, where they enter the substitution rule for several variables, and in multilinear algebra.

For a fixed nonnegative integer n, there is a unique _____ function for the n×n matrices over any commutative ring R. In particular, this function exists when R is the field of real or complex numbers.

a. Package-on-Package
b. Motion Picture Association of America's film-rating system
c. Black Friday
d. Determinant

Chapter 10. Relationship-Based Buying

12. _____ is a service provided by many retailers of various products, primarily electronics, that provides the end-user with a resource for information regarding the product, and help if the product should malfunction. _____ can be found in most manuals for products in the form of a phone number, website address, or physical location.

The Internet has allowed for a new form of _____ to develop.

   a. Product life cycle
   b. Psychological pricing
   c. Price-weighted
   d. Product support

13. _____ refers to planned and systematic production processes that provide confidence in a product's suitability for its intended purpose. Refer to the definition by Merriam-Webster for further information. It is a set of activities intended to ensure that products (goods and/or services) satisfy customer requirements in a systematic, reliable fashion.
   a. 6-3-5 Brainwriting
   b. 180SearchAssistant
   c. Power III
   d. Quality assurance

14. _____ consists of the processes a company uses to track and organize its contacts with its current and prospective customers. _____ software is used to support these processes; information about customers and customer interactions can be entered, stored and accessed by employees in different company departments. Typical _____ goals are to improve services provided to customers, and to use customer contact information for targeted marketing.
   a. Product bundling
   b. Customer relationship management
   c. Demand generation
   d. Commercialization

15. _____ can be regarded as an outcome of mental processes (cognitive process) leading to the selection of a course of action among several alternatives. Every _____ process produces a final choice. The output can be an action or an opinion of choice.
   a. 180SearchAssistant
   b. Decision making
   c. Power III
   d. 6-3-5 Brainwriting

16. Customer _____ consists of the processes a company uses to track and organize its contacts with its current and prospective customers. CRelationship management software is used to support these processes; information about customers and customer interactions can be entered, stored and accessed by employees in different company departments. Typical CRelationship management goals are to improve services provided to customers, and to use customer contact information for targeted marketing.
   a. Marketing
   b. Green marketing
   c. Product bundling
   d. Relationship management

Chapter 11. Customer Loyalty to Products, Brands, and Stores

1. The loyalty business model is a business model used in strategic management in which company resources are employed so as to increase the loyalty of customers and other stakeholders in the expectation that corporate objectives will be met or surpassed. A typical example of this type of model is: quality of product or service leads to customer satisfaction, which leads to _____, which leads to profitability.

Fredrick Reichheld (1996) expanded the loyalty business model beyond customers and employees.

   a. 6-3-5 Brainwriting
   b. 180SearchAssistant
   c. Power III
   d. Customer loyalty

2. A _____ is a collection of symbols, experiences and associations connected with a product, a service, a person or any other artifact or entity.

_____s have become increasingly important components of culture and the economy, now being described as 'cultural accessories and personal philosophies'.

Some people distinguish the psychological aspect of a _____ from the experiential aspect.

   a. Brand equity
   b. Store brand
   c. Brand
   d. Brandable software

3. In environmental modeling and especially in hydrology, a _____ model means a model that is acceptably consistent with observed natural processes, i.e. that simulates well, for example, observed river discharge. It is a key concept of the so-called Generalized Likelihood Uncertainty Estimation (GLUE) methodology to quantify how uncertain environmental predictions are.
   a. 6-3-5 Brainwriting
   b. Power III
   c. 180SearchAssistant
   d. Behavioral

4. _____, in marketing, consists of a consumer's commitment to repurchase the brand and can be demonstrated by repeated buying of a product or service or other positive behaviors such as word of mouth advocacy. True _____ implies that the consumer is willing, at least on occasion, to put aside their own desires in the interest of the brand. _____ has been proclaimed by some to be the ultimate goal of marketing.

Chapter 11. Customer Loyalty to Products, Brands, and Stores

a. Brand awareness
b. Trade Symbols
c. Brand loyalty
d. Brand implementation

5. _____ is a way of expressing knowledge or belief that an event will occur or has occurred. In mathematics the concept has been given an exact meaning in _____ theory, that is used extensively in such areas of study as mathematics, statistics, finance, gambling, science, and philosophy to draw conclusions about the likelihood of potential events and the underlying mechanics of complex systems.

a. Heteroskedastic
b. Linear regression
c. Data
d. Probability

6. _____ is an advertisement in which a particular product specifically mentions a competitor by name for the express purpose of showing why the competitor is inferior to the product naming it.

This should not be confused with parody advertisements, where a fictional product is being advertised for the purpose of poking fun at the particular advertisement, nor should it be confused with the use of a coined brand name for the purpose of comparing the product without actually naming an actual competitor. ('Wikipedia tastes better and is less filling than the Encyclopedia Galactica.')

In the 1980s, during what has been referred to as the cola wars, soft-drink manufacturer Pepsi ran a series of advertisements where people, caught on hidden camera, in a blind taste test, chose Pepsi over rival Coca-Cola.

a. Comparative advertising
b. Heavy-up
c. Cost per conversion
d. GL-70

7. _____ is the perception of the customers that all brands are equivalent (Paul S. Richardson, Alan S. Dick and Arun K. Jain 'Extrinsic and Intrinsic Cue Effects on Perceptions of Store Brand Quality', Journal of Marketing Oct.1994 pp. 28-36) .

a. Line extension
b. Demonstrator model
c. Brand parity
d. Product planning

8. Competitiveness is a comparative concept of the ability and performance of a firm, sub-sector or country to sell and supply goods and/or services in a given market. Although widely used in economics and business management, the usefulness of the concept, particularly in the context of national competitiveness, is vigorously disputed by economists, such as Paul Krugman.

The term may also be applied to markets, where it is used to refer to the extent to which the market structure may be regarded as perfectly _____.

a. Competitive
b. Geographical pricing
c. Free trade zone
d. Customs union

9. _____ refers to the marketing effects or outcomes that accrue to a product with its brand name compared with those that would accrue if the same product did not have the brand name. And, at the root of these marketing effects is consumers' knowledge. In other words, consumers' knowledge about a brand makes manufacturers/advertisers respond differently or adopt appropriately adapt measures for the marketing of the brand.

a. Brand aversion
b. Brand equity
c. Product extension
d. Brand image

10. Merchandising refers to the methods, practices and operations conducted to promote and sustain certain categories of commercial activity. The term is understood to have different specific meanings depending on the context. _____ is a sale goods at a store

In marketing, one of the definitions of merchandising is the practice in which the brand or image from one product or service is used to sell another.

a. New Media Strategies
b. Merchandising
c. Sales promotion
d. Merchandise

11. _____ in economics and business is the result of an exchange and from that trade we assign a numerical monetary value to a good, service or asset. If I trade 4 apples for an orange, the _____ of an orange is 4 - apples. Inversely, the _____ of an apple is 1/4 oranges.

a. Price
b. Discounts and allowances
c. Contribution margin-based pricing
d. Pricing

12. A personal and cultural _____ is a relative ethic _____, an assumption upon which implementation can be extrapolated. A _____ system is a set of consistent _____s and measures that is soo not true. A principle _____ is a foundation upon which other _____s and measures of integrity are based.
   a. Package-on-Package
   b. Perceptual maps
   c. Supreme Court of the United States
   d. Value

13. _____ is anything that is intended to save time, energy or frustration. A _____ store at a petrol station, for example, sells items that have nothing to do with gasoline/petrol, but it saves the consumer from having to go to a grocery store. '_____' is a very relative term and its meaning tends to change over time.
   a. Demographic profile
   b. Convenience
   c. MaxDiff
   d. Marketing buzz

14. _____s (house brands in the United States, own brands in the UK, and home brands in Australia) are brands which are specific to a retail store or store chain. The retailer can manufacture goods under its own label, re-brand private label goods, or outsource manufacture of _____ items to multiple third parties - often the same manufacturers that produce brand label goods. _____ goods are generally cheaper than national brand goods because the retailer can optimize the production to suit consumer demand and reduce advertising costs.
   a. Store brand
   b. Brand strength analysis
   c. Brand loyalty
   d. Brand ambassador

15. In algebra, a _____ is a function depending on n that associates a scalar, det(A), to an n×n square matrix A. The fundamental geometric meaning of a _____ is a scale factor for measure when A is regarded as a linear transformation. _____s are important both in calculus, where they enter the substitution rule for several variables, and in multilinear algebra.

For a fixed nonnegative integer n, there is a unique _____ function for the n×n matrices over any commutative ring R. In particular, this function exists when R is the field of real or complex numbers.

Chapter 11. Customer Loyalty to Products, Brands, and Stores

a. Black Friday
b. Determinant
c. Package-on-Package
d. Motion Picture Association of America's film-rating system

16. _____ or personalisation is tailoring a consumer product, electronic or written medium to a user based on personal details or characteristics they provide. More recently, it has especially been applied in the context of the World Wide Web.

Web pages are personalized based on the interests of an individual.

a. Personalization
b. Sexism,
c. Flighting
d. Complex sale

17. An _____ is an unplanned or otherwise spontaneous purchase. One who tends to make such purchases is referred to as an impulse purchaser or impulse buyer.

Marketers and retailers tend to exploit these impulses which are tied to the basic want for instant gratification.

a. AMAX
b. ADTECH
c. ACNielsen
d. Impulse purchase

18. _____ is the examining of goods or services from retailers with the intent to purchase at that time. _____ is an activity of selection and/or purchase. In some contexts it is considered a leisure activity as well as an economic one.

a. Hawkers
b. Discount store
c. Khodebshchik
d. Shopping

19. _____ is the set of reasons that determines one to engage in a particular behavior. The term is generally used for human _____ but, theoretically, it can be used to describe the causes for animal behavior as well

Chapter 11. Customer Loyalty to Products, Brands, and Stores

a. Role playing
b. Power III
c. 180SearchAssistant
d. Motivation

20. _____ is a concept that denotes the precise probability of specific eventualities. Technically, the notion of _____ is independent from the notion of value and, as such, eventualities may have both beneficial and adverse consequences. However, in general usage the convention is to focus only on potential negative impact to some characteristic of value that may arise from a future event.
a. 180SearchAssistant
b. Power III
c. 6-3-5 Brainwriting
d. Risk

21. _____ can be regarded as an outcome of mental processes (cognitive process) leading to the selection of a course of action among several alternatives. Every _____ process produces a final choice. The output can be an action or an opinion of choice.
a. 6-3-5 Brainwriting
b. Power III
c. 180SearchAssistant
d. Decision making

22. The _____ is a trilateral trade bloc in North America created by the governments of the United States, Canada, and Mexico. It superseded the Canada-United States Free Trade Agreement between the US and Canada.

Following diplomatic negotiations dating back to 1990 between the three nations, the leaders met in San Antonio, Texas on December 17, 1992 to sign _____.

a. Power III
b. 6-3-5 Brainwriting
c. North American Free Trade Agreement
d. 180SearchAssistant

23. _____, a business term, is a measure of how products and services supplied by a company meet or surpass customer expectation. It is seen as a key performance indicator within business and is part of the four perspectives of a Balanced Scorecard.

In a competitive marketplace where businesses compete for customers, _____ is seen as a key differentiator and increasingly has become a key element of business strategy.

   a. Supplier diversity
   b. Customer satisfaction
   c. Customer base
   d. Psychological pricing

Chapter 12. Online Customer Behavior

1. _____ is the study of when, why, how, where and what people do or do not buy products. It blends elements from psychology, sociology, social psychology, anthropology and economics. It attempts to understand the buyer decision making process, both individually and in groups. It studies characteristics of individual consumers such as demographics and behavioural variables in an attempt to understand people's wants. It also tries to assess influences on the consumer from groups such as family, friends, reference groups, and society in general.
   a. Communal marketing
   b. Multidimensional scaling
   c. Consumer confidence
   d. Consumer behavior

2. Electronic commerce, commonly known as _____ or eCommerce, consists of the buying and selling of products or services over electronic systems such as the Internet and other computer networks. The amount of trade conducted electronically has grown extraordinarily with wide-spread Internet usage. A wide variety of commerce is conducted in this way, spurring and drawing on innovations in electronic funds transfer, supply chain management, Internet marketing, online transaction processing, electronic data interchange (EDI), inventory management systems, and automated data collection systems.
   a. AMAX
   b. E-commerce
   c. ADTECH
   d. ACNielsen

3. The _____ is a very large set of interlinked hypertext documents accessed via the Internet. With a Web browser, one can view Web pages that may contain text, images, videos, and other multimedia and navigate between them using hyperlinks. Using concepts from earlier hypertext systems, the _____ was begun in 1992 by the English physicist Sir Tim Berners-Lee, now the Director of the _____ Consortium, and Robert Cailliau, a Belgian computer scientist, while both were working at CERN in Geneva, Switzerland.
   a. 6-3-5 Brainwriting
   b. 180SearchAssistant
   c. Power III
   d. World Wide Web

4. _____ is difficult to define. For example, in 1952, Alfred Kroeber and Clyde Kluckhohn compiled a list of 164 definitions of '_____' in _____: A Critical Review of Concepts and Definitions. However, the word '_____' is most commonly used in three basic senses:

   - excellence of taste in the fine arts and humanities
   - an integrated pattern of human knowledge, belief, and behavior that depends upon the capacity for symbolic thought and social learning
   - the set of shared attitudes, values, goals, and practices that characterizes an institution, organization or group.

When the concept first emerged in eighteenth- and nineteenth-century Europe, it connoted a process of cultivation or improvement, as in agriculture or horticulture. In the nineteenth century, it came to refer first to the betterment or refinement of the individual, especially through education, and then to the fulfillment of national aspirations or ideals.

a. African Americans
b. Albert Einstein
c. AStore
d. Culture

5. _____ is an advertisement in which a particular product specifically mentions a competitor by name for the express purpose of showing why the competitor is inferior to the product naming it.

This should not be confused with parody advertisements, where a fictional product is being advertised for the purpose of poking fun at the particular advertisement, nor should it be confused with the use of a coined brand name for the purpose of comparing the product without actually naming an actual competitor. ('Wikipedia tastes better and is less filling than the Encyclopedia Galactica.')

In the 1980s, during what has been referred to as the cola wars, soft-drink manufacturer Pepsi ran a series of advertisements where people, caught on hidden camera, in a blind taste test, chose Pepsi over rival Coca-Cola.

a. Cost per conversion
b. Comparative advertising
c. Heavy-up
d. GL-70

6. _____ can be regarded as an outcome of mental processes (cognitive process) leading to the selection of a course of action among several alternatives. Every _____ process produces a final choice. The output can be an action or an opinion of choice.

a. 6-3-5 Brainwriting
b. Decision making
c. Power III
d. 180SearchAssistant

Chapter 12. Online Customer Behavior

7. _____ is a recursive process where two or more people or organizations work together toward an intersection of common goals -- for example, an intellectual endeavor that is creative in nature--by sharing knowledge, learning and building consensus. _____ does not require leadership and can sometimes bring better results through decentralization and egalitarianism. In particular, teams that work collaboratively can obtain greater resources, recognition and reward when facing competition for finite resources._____ is also present in opposing goals exhibiting the notion of adversarial _____, though this notion is atypical of the annotation that people have given towards their understanding of _____.
   a. Power III
   b. Collaboration
   c. 180SearchAssistant
   d. 6-3-5 Brainwriting

8. _____ is the process of filtering for information or patterns using techniques involving collaboration among multiple agents, viewpoints, data sources, etc. Applications of _____ typically involve very large data sets. _____ methods have been applied to many different kinds of data including sensing and monitoring data - such as in mineral exploration, environmental sensing over large areas or multiple sensors; financial data - such as financial service institutions that integrate many financial sources; or in electronic commerce and web 2.0 applications where the focus is on user data, etc.
   a. 180SearchAssistant
   b. 6-3-5 Brainwriting
   c. Collaborative filtering
   d. Power III

9. _____s form a specific type of information filtering (IF) technique that attempts to present information items (movies, music, books, news, images, web pages, etc.) that are likely of interest to the user. Typically, a _____ compares the user's profile to some reference characteristics, and seeks to predict the 'rating' that a user would give to an item they had not yet considered.
   a. Permission marketing
   b. Locator software
   c. Spamvertising
   d. Recommender system

10. _____ is systematic determination of merit, worth, and significance of something or someone using criteria against a set of standards. _____ often is used to characterize and appraise subjects of interest in a wide range of human enterprises, including the arts, criminal justice, foundations and non-profit organizations, government, health care, and other human services.

Depending on the topic of interest, there are professional groups which look to the quality and rigor of the _____ process.

a. AMAX
b. ADTECH
c. ACNielsen
d. Evaluation

11. _____s are Web-based intelligent software applications that can help online shoppers find lower price for commodities or services. Price comparison services was the earliest service a _____ provides. To search the price of a particular item, a _____ would search multiple online stores based on the keyword the online shopper provides.

a. Distribution
b. Comparison-Shopping agent
c. Book of business
d. Net Promoter^R score

12. _____ is a neologism, defined as the combination of operational customization and marketing customization.

_____ is considered one of the key drivers underpinning the new economy. Most companies today are changing their marketing model from a seller-centric to a buyer-centric one.

a. Market intelligence
b. Product planning
c. Targeted advertising
d. Customerization

13. _____ or personalisation is tailoring a consumer product, electronic or written medium to a user based on personal details or characteristics they provide. More recently, it has especially been applied in the context of the World Wide Web.

Web pages are personalized based on the interests of an individual.

a. Flighting
b. Sexism,
c. Personalization
d. Complex sale

14. _____ is the ability of an individual or group to seclude themselves or information about themselves and thereby reveal themselves selectively. The boundaries and content of what is considered private differ among cultures and individuals, but share basic common themes. _____ is sometimes related to anonymity, the wish to remain unnoticed or unidentified in the public realm.

a. 180SearchAssistant
b. 6-3-5 Brainwriting
c. Power III
d. Privacy

15. _____ is the price at which an asset would trade in a competitive Walrasian auction setting. _____ is often used interchangeably with open _____, fair value or fair _____, although these terms have distinct definitions in different standards, and may differ in some circumstances.

International Valuation Standards defines _____ as 'the estimated amount for which a property should exchange on the date of valuation between a willing buyer and a willing seller in an arm's-length transaction after proper marketing wherein the parties had each acted knowledgeably, prudently, and without compulsion.'

_____ is a concept distinct from market price, which is 'the price at which one can transact', while _____ is 'the true underlying value' according to theoretical standards.

a. Market value
b. Power III
c. 180SearchAssistant
d. Restructuring

16. A personal and cultural _____ is a relative ethic _____, an assumption upon which implementation can be extrapolated. A _____ system is a set of consistent _____s and measures that is soo not true. A principle _____ is a foundation upon which other _____s and measures of integrity are based.
a. Package-on-Package
b. Supreme Court of the United States
c. Perceptual maps
d. Value

17. _____ refers to a business or organization attempting to acquire goods or services to accomplish the goals of the enterprise. Though there are several organizations that attempt to set standards in the _____ process, processes can vary greatly between organizations. Typically the word '_____' is not used interchangeably with the word 'procurement', since procurement typically includes Expediting, Supplier Quality, and Traffic and Logistics (T'L) in addition to _____.
a. Supply chain
b. Supply network
c. Drop shipping
d. Purchasing

18. _____ is a term used to describe practice of sourcing from the global market for goods and services across geopolitical boundaries. _____ often aims to exploit global efficiencies in the delivery of a product or service. These efficiencies include low cost skilled labor, low cost raw material and other economic factors like tax breaks and low trade tariffs.

   a. Power III
   b. 6-3-5 Brainwriting
   c. 180SearchAssistant
   d. Global sourcing

19. A _____ is the space, actual or metaphorical, in which a market operates. The term is also used in a trademark law context to denote the actual consumer environment, ie. the 'real world' in which products and services are provided and consumed.

   a. Marketplace
   b. 6-3-5 Brainwriting
   c. Power III
   d. 180SearchAssistant

20. A _____ is a framework for creating economic, social, and/or other forms of value. The term _____ is thus used for a broad range of informal and formal descriptions to represent core aspects of a business, including purpose, offerings, strategies, infrastructure, organizational structures, trading practices, and operational processes and policies.

   In the most basic sense, a _____ is the method of doing business by which a company can sustain itself -- that is, generate revenue.

   a. Service provider
   b. Business model
   c. Pay to surf
   d. Yield management

21. _____ is a broad label that refers to any individuals or households that use goods and services generated within the economy. The concept of a _____ is used in different contexts, so that the usage and significance of the term may vary.

   A _____ is a person who uses any product or service.

a. Consumer
b. Power III
c. 180SearchAssistant
d. 6-3-5 Brainwriting

22. _____ is the business-to-business or business-to-consumer or Business-to-government purchase and sale of supplies, Work and services through the Internet as well as other information and networking systems, such as Electronic Data Interchange and Enterprise Resource Planning. Typically, _____ Web sites allow qualified and registered users to look for buyers or sellers of goods and services. Depending on the approach, buyers or sellers may specify costs or invite bids.

a. ADTECH
b. ACNielsen
c. AMAX
d. E-procurement

23. _____ is the ability to conduct commerce, using a mobile device e.g. a mobile phone, a PDA, a smartphone and other emerging mobile equipment such as dashtop mobile devices. _____ has been defined as follows:

'_____ is any transaction, involving the transfer of ownership or rights to use goods and services, which is initiated and/or completed by using mobile access to computer-mediated networks with the help of an electronic device.'

In 2000 and 2001 hundreds of billions of dollars in licensing fees were paid by European telecommunications companies for UMTS and other 3G licenses. The high prices paid were due to the expectation of highly profitable _____ applications.

a. Mobile commerce
b. Web banner
c. Business-to-government
d. Consumer privacy

Chapter 13. Creating Market Values for the Customer

1. _____ is the price at which an asset would trade in a competitive Walrasian auction setting. _____ is often used interchangeably with open _____, fair value or fair _____, although these terms have distinct definitions in different standards, and may differ in some circumstances.

   International Valuation Standards defines _____ as 'the estimated amount for which a property should exchange on the date of valuation between a willing buyer and a willing seller in an arm's-length transaction after proper marketing wherein the parties had each acted knowledgeably, prudently, and without compulsion.'

   _____ is a concept distinct from market price, which is 'the price at which one can transact', while _____ is 'the true underlying value' according to theoretical standards.

   a. Market value
   b. Power III
   c. 180SearchAssistant
   d. Restructuring

2. A personal and cultural _____ is a relative ethic _____, an assumption upon which implementation can be extrapolated. A _____ system is a set of consistent _____s and measures that is soo not true. A principle _____ is a foundation upon which other _____s and measures of integrity are based.
   a. Package-on-Package
   b. Perceptual maps
   c. Supreme Court of the United States
   d. Value

3. Quality management can be considered to have three main components: quality control, quality assurance and _____. Quality management is focused not only on product quality, but also the means to achieve it. Quality management therefore uses quality assurance and control of processes as well as products to achieve more consistent quality.
   a. Quality improvement
   b. Power III
   c. 6-3-5 Brainwriting
   d. 180SearchAssistant

4. _____ is a market coverage strategy in which a firm decides to ignore market segment differences and go after the whole market with one offer.it is type of marketing (or attempting to sell through persuasion) of a product to a wide audience. The idea is to broadcast a message that will reach the largest number of people possible. Traditionally _____ has focused on radio, television and newspapers as the medium used to reach this broad audience.

Chapter 13. Creating Market Values for the Customer

a. Business-to-consumer
b. Mass marketing
c. Marketspace
d. Cyberdoc

5. _____, in marketing, manufacturing, and management, is the use of flexible computer-aided manufacturing systems to produce custom output. Those systems combine the low unit costs of mass production processes with the flexibility of individual customization.

'_____' is the new frontier in business competition for both manufacturing and service industries.

a. Vertical integration
b. Mass customization
c. Power III
d. Flanking marketing warfare strategies

6. An _____ is quite usually a standard guarantee from the seller of a product that specifies the extent to which the quality or performance of the product is assured and states the conditions under which the product can be returned, replaced, or repaired. It is often given in the form of a specific, written 'Warranty' document. However, a warranty may also arise by operation of law based upon the seller's description of the goods, and perhaps their source and quality, and any material deviation from that specification would violate the guarantee.
a. Express warranty
b. Energy Star
c. Imperial Group v. Philip Morris
d. Office for Harmonization in the Internal Market

7. On an intranet or B2E Enterprise Web portals, personalization is often based on user attributes such as department, functional area, or role. The term _____ in this context refers to the ability of users to modify the page layout or specify what content should be displayed.

There are two categories of personalizations:

1. Rule-based
2. Content-based

Web personalization models include rules-based filtering, based on 'if this, then that' rules processing, and collaborative filtering, which serves relevant material to customers by combining their own personal preferences with the preferences of like-minded others. Collaborative filtering works well for books, music, video, etc.

Chapter 13. Creating Market Values for the Customer

a. Customization
b. Movin'
c. Cashmere Agency
d. Self branding

8. _____ is one of the four Ps of the marketing mix. The other three aspects are product, promotion, and place. It is also a key variable in microeconomic price allocation theory.

a. Price
b. Competitor indexing
c. Relationship based pricing
d. Pricing

9. A _____ is a collection of symbols, experiences and associations connected with a product, a service, a person or any other artifact or entity.

_____s have become increasingly important components of culture and the economy, now being described as 'cultural accessories and personal philosophies'.

Some people distinguish the psychological aspect of a _____ from the experiential aspect.

a. Store brand
b. Brand equity
c. Brandable software
d. Brand

10. _____ is defined by the American _____ Association as the activity, set of institutions, and processes for creating, communicating, delivering, and exchanging offerings that have value for customers, clients, partners, and society at large. The term developed from the original meaning which referred literally to going to market, as in shopping, or going to a market to sell goods or services.

_____ practice tends to be seen as a creative industry, which includes advertising, distribution and selling.

a. Customer acquisition management
b. Marketing myopia
c. Marketing
d. Product naming

Chapter 13. Creating Market Values for the Customer

11. _____ or cause-related marketing refers to a type of marketing involving the cooperative efforts of a 'for profit' business and a non-profit organization for mutual benefit. The term is sometimes used more broadly and generally to refer to any type of marketing effort for social and other charitable causes, including in-house marketing efforts by non-profit organizations. _____ differs from corporate giving (philanthropy) as the latter generally involves a specific donation that is tax deductible, while _____ is a marketing relationship generally not based on a donation.
    a. Cause-related Marketing
    b. Digital marketing
    c. Global marketing
    d. Cause marketing

12. _____ refers to messages and related media used to communicate with a market. Those who practice advertising, branding, direct marketing, graphic design, marketing, packaging, promotion, publicity, sponsorship, public relations, sales, sales promotion and online marketing are termed marketing communicators, _____ managers, or more briefly as marcom managers.
    a. Merchandise
    b. Merchandising
    c. Sales promotion
    d. Marketing communication

13. _____ in economics and business is the result of an exchange and from that trade we assign a numerical monetary value to a good, service or asset. If I trade 4 apples for an orange, the _____ of an orange is 4 - apples. Inversely, the _____ of an apple is 1/4 oranges.
    a. Discounts and allowances
    b. Pricing
    c. Contribution margin-based pricing
    d. Price

14. _____ in economics refers to metrics and measures of output from production processes, per unit of input. Labor _____, for example, is typically measured as a ratio of output per labor-hour, an input. _____ may be conceived of as a metrics of the technical or engineering efficiency of production.
    a. Power III
    b. Value engineering
    c. 180SearchAssistant
    d. Productivity

15. _____, in microeconomics, are the cost advantages that a business obtains due to expansion. They are factors that cause a producer's average cost per unit to fall as output rises. Diseconomies of scale are the opposite.

Chapter 13. Creating Market Values for the Customer

a. AMAX
b. ACNielsen
c. ADTECH
d. Economies of scale

16. _____ is, in computer science and management, an approach aiming at improvements by means of elevating efficiency and effectiveness of the business process that exist within and across organizations. The key to _____ is for organizations to look at their business processes from a 'clean slate' perspective and determine how they can best construct these processes to improve how they conduct business. _____ Cycle.

_____ is also known as _____, Business Process Redesign, Business Transformation, or Business Process Change Management.

a. Customer retention
b. Price-weighted
c. Supplier diversity
d. Business process reengineering

17. _____ is the state or fact of exclusive rights and control over property, which may be an object, land/real estate, or some other kind of property (like government-granted monopolies collectively referred to as intellectual property.) It is embodied in an _____ right also referred to as title.

_____ is the key building block in the development of the capitalist socio-economic system.

a. AMAX
b. ACNielsen
c. ADTECH
d. Ownership

18. _____ is an advertisement in which a particular product specifically mentions a competitor by name for the express purpose of showing why the competitor is inferior to the product naming it.

This should not be confused with parody advertisements, where a fictional product is being advertised for the purpose of poking fun at the particular advertisement, nor should it be confused with the use of a coined brand name for the purpose of comparing the product without actually naming an actual competitor. ('Wikipedia tastes better and is less filling than the Encyclopedia Galactica.')

In the 1980s, during what has been referred to as the cola wars, soft-drink manufacturer Pepsi ran a series of advertisements where people, caught on hidden camera, in a blind taste test, chose Pepsi over rival Coca-Cola.

a. Heavy-up
b. GL-70
c. Comparative advertising
d. Cost per conversion

19. In economics, _____ is a measure of the relative satisfaction from consumption of various goods and services. Given this measure, one may speak meaningfully of increasing or decreasing _____, and thereby explain economic behavior in terms of attempts to increase one's _____. For illustrative purposes, changes in _____ are sometimes expressed in units called utils.

a. ACNielsen
b. AMAX
c. Utility
d. ADTECH

20. _____ is anything that is intended to save time, energy or frustration. A _____ store at a petrol station, for example, sells items that have nothing to do with gasoline/petrol, but it saves the consumer from having to go to a grocery store. '_____' is a very relative term and its meaning tends to change over time.

a. Demographic profile
b. Marketing buzz
c. MaxDiff
d. Convenience

21. _____ or personalisation is tailoring a consumer product, electronic or written medium to a user based on personal details or characteristics they provide. More recently, it has especially been applied in the context of the World Wide Web.

Web pages are personalized based on the interests of an individual.

a. Sexism,
b. Personalization
c. Flighting
d. Complex sale

22. In psychology, philosophy, and the cognitive sciences, _____ is the process of attaining awareness or understanding of sensory information. It is a task far more complex than was imagined in the 1950s and 1960s, when it was predicted that building perceiving machines would take about a decade, a goal which is still very far from fruition. The word _____ comes from the Latin words _____, percepio, meaning 'receiving, collecting, action of taking possession, apprehension with the mind or senses.'

_____ is one of the oldest fields in psychology.

a. Groupthink
b. 180SearchAssistant
c. Power III
d. Perception

ANSWER KEY

Chapter 1
1. c   2. c   3. d   4. b   5. a   6. b   7. d   8. d   9. d   10. b
11. a   12. d   13. d   14. d   15. d   16. a   17. c   18. b   19. b   20. d
21. b   22. d   23. c   24. a   25. c   26. c

Chapter 2
1. d   2. d   3. d   4. b   5. a   6. d   7. b   8. b   9. d   10. a
11. b   12. c   13. d   14. b   15. a   16. d   17. d   18. d   19. c   20. a
21. c   22. c   23. a   24. d   25. d   26. c   27. d   28. d   29. c   30. d
31. d   32. d   33. d   34. d   35. a   36. d   37. d   38. d   39. b   40. d
41. c   42. d   43. d   44. d

Chapter 3
1. c   2. d   3. c   4. a   5. d   6. a   7. b   8. c   9. d   10. b
11. a   12. c   13. b   14. d   15. d   16. d   17. a   18. a   19. c   20. d
21. a   22. c   23. d   24. d   25. a   26. c

Chapter 4
1. b   2. a   3. d   4. d   5. d   6. d   7. a   8. c   9. c   10. c
11. d   12. d   13. a   14. d   15. c   16. c   17. d   18. d   19. b   20. d
21. d   22. b   23. a   24. d   25. b   26. d

Chapter 5
1. a   2. c   3. b   4. c   5. a   6. b   7. d   8. a   9. d   10. b
11. b   12. a   13. d   14. b   15. d   16. d   17. a   18. d   19. c   20. d
21. c   22. d

Chapter 6
1. a   2. a   3. d   4. b   5. d   6. c   7. c   8. b   9. b   10. c
11. c   12. d   13. a   14. d   15. d   16. d   17. b

Chapter 7
1. d   2. d   3. a   4. b   5. c   6. d   7. c   8. a   9. d   10. a
11. b   12. d   13. a   14. b   15. d   16. d   17. c   18. c   19. d   20. d
21. d   22. d   23. c   24. b   25. d   26. b   27. c   28. b   29. d   30. b
31. d

Chapter 8
1. c   2. d   3. c   4. d   5. d   6. b   7. b   8. d   9. d   10. c
11. d   12. b   13. c   14. b   15. d   16. c   17. a   18. b   19. c   20. c

Chapter 9
1. c   2. d   3. a   4. a   5. b   6. b   7. a   8. d   9. b   10. d
11. d   12. a   13. d   14. d   15. a   16. b   17. d   18. d   19. a   20. d
21. a   22. d   23. d   24. b   25. a   26. b

ANSWER KEY

Chapter 10
1. d   2. d   3. d   4. d   5. d   6. d   7. d   8. d   9. d   10. d
11. d   12. d   13. d   14. b   15. b   16. d

Chapter 11
1. d   2. c   3. d   4. c   5. d   6. a   7. c   8. a   9. b   10. d
11. a   12. d   13. b   14. a   15. b   16. a   17. d   18. d   19. d   20. d
21. d   22. c   23. b

Chapter 12
1. d   2. b   3. d   4. d   5. b   6. b   7. b   8. c   9. d   10. d
11. b   12. d   13. c   14. d   15. a   16. d   17. d   18. d   19. a   20. b
21. a   22. d   23. a

Chapter 13
1. a   2. d   3. a   4. b   5. b   6. a   7. a   8. d   9. d   10. c
11. d   12. d   13. d   14. d   15. d   16. d   17. d   18. c   19. c   20. d
21. b   22. d